CHRIS✝IAN & ENTREPRENEUR

THE GOAL-MIND TO GOD'S GOLD MINE

FIRST EDITION

TIFFANY KAMENI

Christian & Entrepreneur

The Goal-Mind to GOD'S Goldmine

Gold Edition

"The plans of the diligent lead to profit as surely as haste leads to poverty."
Proverbs 21:5 (NIV)

Table of Contents

<u>Introduction</u>

You're Christian and you're an entrepreneur. This combination
alone is powerful because you had to (or have to) learn self-
control and how to apply your lessons in life to your business
and vice-versa. How can you find your way to your Promised
Land, and what's awaiting you when you get there.

Christian & Entrepreneur: The Goal-Mind to GOD'S Goldmine is
a detailed book that will teach you how to access your wealthy
place: your mind! There are many books that are helpful with
guiding the Christian entrepreneur by teaching you how to
manage success once you reach it. This book teaches you how
to tap into the success that is in you, and how to start operating
in that mindset today.

Understand that there is a difference between running a
Christian business and running a successful Christian business.
They are not one in the same, and the difference between the
two is worlds apart. That's why many Christians start and
close businesses at record speeds.

Let's say that GOD gave you a business to start and you want to
get it off the ground. Did you know that a pilot must first
possess the knowledge of how to fly a plane before he takes to

the skies in that plane? If he doesn't get this knowledge, he will undoubtedly crash. Business ownership works the same way. In order to get your business off the ground, you have to get the necessary knowledge of how to run and maintain your company before you start it. Running out there with an idea and a website simply isn't enough. You need the fear of GOD, the mind of an entrepreneur, and the patience of a spider. The knowledge you acquire is like a web that you have spawn and this web is designed to catch every blessing that GOD sends your way.

Learn from Tiffany Kameni, the founder of Anointed Fire™, one of today's most successful Christian establishments. With no college education, no money, and no idea how to start a business, Tiffany Kameni sat down and was obedient to the voice of the HOLY SPIRIT. She learned how to view and access the success that GOD had planted on the inside of her. Through obedience, trial, and error; Tiffany Kameni built an empire from the comfort of her own home.

As a business coach, Tiffany Kameni now instructs business owners how to access the success that GOD has instilled in them.

In this book, you will discover how to take what GOD has placed on the inside of you and make it work on the outside. You will learn how to tap into your anointing, and how to make it work for you. So many Christian business owners close their businesses because they never availed themselves to obtain the knowledge that is available to them. This book talks about the inner-workings of running a Christian business, what to expect, and how to bypass the obstacles that have stopped so many Christian entrepreneurs from advancing.

You would be amazed to find out that greatness is in you, but the world has corrupted the believer so that they too have trouble accessing it. It's time to break the chains of misunderstanding, lies, and generational mindsets. It's time to power up on the truth and be transformed into the success story that GOD has called you to be. An absolute must read for anyone desiring to walk in the fullness of their entrepreneurial anointing.

Letter From the Author

Dear Future Success Story,

I thought it would be fitting to share with you my testimony and oath to the LORD, and maybe it may inspire you to dedicate your business, your hands and so on to HIM.

One day, I heard the LORD say to me that I was going to build websites. I became overjoyed on the spot and I couldn't wait to jump right into my new gift. Being a baby Christian, I opened a hip-hop website that promoted the enemy's work. I didn't think anything was wrong with it because I'd convinced myself that as long as I didn't play profanity or sexually charged lyrics I was okay. I felt this conviction come over me, but I would often put it to bed with my attempt to justify what I was doing. I begin to design websites for hip-hop artists and before you know it, my name was spiraling around the secular world as an affordable designer. Again, there was that conviction that muscled me around when I uploaded a song to my website or promoted the site itself.

Finally, I went to the LORD about what I was promoting and I waited for HIS answer. One day, one of the artists whom I'd designed for called me and asked me to delete his website. He told me that he'd given himself to the LORD and was giving up rap and hip-hop. He began to tell me about how the LORD had been dealing with him, and I immediately felt that conviction again. Here was the LORD using this man to minister to me without him knowing it. I confessed to him about the LORD dealing with me the same way, and I hurriedly went to the computer and began to delete my hip-hop website. I knew that if I didn't do it, I would find some reason to not do it later.

The backlash behind my decision was heavy. There were many who thought that I was three miles past stupid, because my site had been taking off in the hip-hop world. I didn't care though. I wanted so desperately to please the LORD, and this has been my wholehearted desire every since.

As I began my journey working for HIM, I had to commit my hands and my heart to HIM. I told HIM that I would never prostitute my gifts again. I would never build for the kingdom of darkness, but I would build for HIS Kingdom only. What an amazing GOD we serve, for HE is forgiving and merciful. I had to start over from the bottom and faith my way on up.

One day, I decided that I wanted to play around with making logos. The designs were pretty good for a first-timer. I began to market them online, and I got a few orders to start off. One of my clients asked me if I knew how to design seals, and I didn't know what a seal was, so I Googled it. It looked like the logos I'd been creating, so I agreed to do the work. After I finished, I sent him a copy of the design with the word "sample" stamped on it. I was chasing the money and desperate to get some extra cash, but he started saying that he'd given the money to his secretary to give to me. As the days passed, I began to grow impatient because I'd already told my husband about this money, and I was determined to help out around the house with the bills. Finally, I called the client and told him that if I didn't have the money by a set time (don't remember it exactly), that I was going to auction it off on Facebook. He was nice about it and apologized for the delay. After he didn't make the payment, I posted it up for sale. $75 was my fee for the design, and I said that the first person that paid for it could have it. Several people inboxed me about it, but one man finally asked me to send him the invoice, and he paid it. I thought that was the end of it, but it wasn't. I continued to get messages asking me my prices, and I began to get orders behind orders. It was all a setup from the LORD! HE'D arranged this to happen to create an avenue of income for me and to just bless HIS daughter.

As time went on, there were days when I needed some extra cash, and someone from the world of hip-hop would contact me about a website or a logo. Nevertheless, I had to turn them away to honor my oath to GOD. It felt great to see myself committing my gifts and heart solely to HIM.

Slowly, but surely, my business began to grow and the LORD began to increase my gifts. Suddenly, success overtook me and all of the blessings of GOD began to surround me. I still feel the joy, love and awe when I think about how HE did this for me.

Since then, I have gone on to open up a fully functional graphic design company, a publishing company, I've written several books and launched many businesses. I also help others to launch their Christian businesses by sharing with them what I'm about to share with you. And get this; I have never went to college. I say that to share with you that GOD will bless you if you will honor HIM in your business. The people that I have seen fail all have one thing in common: they honor money and not GOD; or they trust in their degrees, but not GOD. This book is a treasure trove of wisdom, knowledge and understanding that will serve as a life-changing tool if you'll only apply what is taught here.

Again, I have seen the rise, and I have seen the fall of many companies launched by normal people like yourself. Each time,

I could see the bull-dozing barrier that tore the company down, and it was always yielded by the unknowledgeable business owner. In this book, you will come face-to-face with the whales that swallowed these businesses and many Christian businesses whole. You will learn how to avoid them and recognize them. Much of this advice is unconventional, but it is invaluable knowledge that the LORD has taught me through HIS WORD and experience.

Your Sister in CHRIST,
Tiffany Kameni

The Christian Entrepreneur

Entrepreneur (French word): one who organizes, manages, and assumes the risks of a business or enterprise. (Merriam-Webster) Entreprende (Old French): to begin something, undertake. (Wiktionary)
Entre (Latin): Inter or between. (Wiktionary)
Prende: To take. (Wiktionary)

As you can see, the word "entrepreneur" is suitable in describing a business owner. A business owner undertakes or assumes the responsibilities of starting and running a business. These responsibilities include, and are not limited to:
- Financial responsibilities and risks.
- Legal responsibilities and risks.
- Moral responsibilities and risks.
- Spiritual responsibilities and risks.

Every business that opens will have an impact on someone or something. This is the reason that someone has to take on the responsibility of running that business and making sure that it does not have a negative impact on any individual or society as a whole. As a business owner, you run the risk of losing your investment, being sued, incarcerated (if your business harms anyone), shunned, and so on. These responsibilities alone have scared off many would-be business owners. Many entrepreneurs have exited the realm of entrepreneurship just as fast as they'd entered it when they came face-to-face with the responsibilities associated with business ownership. The biggest and scariest responsibility for most is the financial responsibility and risks involved, because running and starting a successful business usually requires a substantial investment. No, you don't have to invest your life's savings, but you are required to make a sacrifice, and sacrifices don't go unnoticed. All the same, many see this investment as a gamble. In truth, if GOD gave you that business idea, you aren't running a gamble in obeying HIM. The real gamble is disobeying HIM.

As a Christian entrepreneur, one of the biggest challenges is finding a market that suits you and does not oppose your Christian values. Let's face it; every one can earn a buck doing just about anything, but what good is it to gain the world and lose one's soul? (See Mark 8:36)

The second greatest challenge is accepting one's role as an entrepreneur. The title itself has a positive ring to it, but it can be intimidating for most. That's because we have come to associate the word "entrepreneur" with great wealth, and if we don't have that wealth yet, we are oftentimes afraid to wear the title.

Overall, the most challenging obstacle is one's relationship with money. People don't like to part with their money unless they are given something in return, but with business ownership (and any investment for that matter), seeing a return on one's investments can take years. This is where patience and faith has to come in to console the believer as they part with the very thing they have to come to depend on. This brings us to our next point.

Do you know why GOD has given you a business to start?

Because not only are you called to establish the Kingdom of GOD on the earth, but GOD wants to break that wrongful relationship with money that you may have. Oftentimes, people have a wrongful relationship with money and they don't realize it. They begin to depend on money, and money becomes their god. They serve money by doing whatever it takes to get it into their hands once again. When we have a wrongful relationship with money, we don't want to part with it for any reason.

Business ownership is a great tool for tearing down this perverse relationship, and building you up on the foundation of faith, because business ownership requires that you make an investment. It requires that you part with your money for a time and believe that GOD will bring it back. It requires you to walk into the unknown realm of entrepreneurship looking to bring more out than what you put in. You will either become a business owner or a successful business owner by the choices you make in running your business. There are times when you will be required to sow into your business, and there are times when you will be required to prune away some things and some people from your business. It is a systematic setup that is designed to make you wiser and break away the lies, misconceptions, and yokes that you have learned to live with. It is truthfully a faith walk and a continual test of one's faith, because it requires you to make unexpected moves in the shadow of a day. Having your own business requires you to do things you wouldn't ordinarily do, buy things you wouldn't ordinarily buy, and learn things you wouldn't ordinarily be interested in.

All the same, being a Christian entrepreneur is a revelatory seed that, if cultivated, will teach you a lot about your faith and give you an inside look at what's going on in the Christian church. One of the most heart-wrenching views that I was given was of the idolatrous relationship that many Christians have with money. As you grow and grow in CHRIST, you will see an increase in your business and a decrease in the people around you. You're going to deal with contention from people and the falling away of people that you held dear to your heart. This is because GOD knows how much success you can handle, and HE continues to increase how much you can handle before HE releases it to you. If the people around you haven't been prepped for success, they can't be around you because they won't know how to deal with you or relate to you at your new level in HIM. They'll keep trying to relate to the old you, and they will shun the new and changed creature in CHRIST. This is when you will find that your friends will become your fiends, and they will become dangerous to you and your destiny. It's not because they were never your friend; it is because they were the friend of who you were or who you'd learned to be; but who you are, they want nothing to do with.

A lot of times, when a Christian entrepreneur faces this opposition coupled with the separating of them from their money, they retreat back to their comfort zones where they weren't being opposed. This is a big test that many entrepreneurs fail because success requires that we come in with our minds dressed a certain way. You can't enter success with your old way of thinking. Success has to enter you and evict that old mindset, and then it invites you to live in it. You are required to make a sacrifice in order to kill that idolatrous mindset and to replace it with a heart of faith. All the same, tithing births the same results because tithing helps you to break that dependency on money and depend on GOD for your wants and needs.

Opposition is the opposing of one's position. As an entrepreneur, your position will often be opposed. As a Christian entrepreneur, you will find that a lot of that opposition is coming from within the church. It's not that you're being opposed by Christians from within the church; you will often be opposed by Satanic plants that sit in the church. They are on their job, and they are professionals at what they do.

I remember talking to a new business owner who was thinking about throwing in the towel. She was being opposed, ridiculed, and made to feel worthless by a female Pastor. In my journey, I'd faced this opposition too, and I'd come to learn that this opposing of one's position is to be expected. All the same, I learned how to handle such a soul. Anyhow, she was confused because she kept looking at the woman's title and not her fruit. When she told me what the woman had been saying to her and doing to her, I told her immediately to disassociate from this woman. I recognized that woman's spirit immediately because in my early entrepreneurial journey, I'd met that spirit one too many times. It is a condescending spirit, whereas the person hosting it will make you feel as if:

- You're not good at what you do.
- You need them to get better.
- Your success depends on them and how you handle them.
- You're absolutely evil for charging them what you charge them. After all, they prophesied to you.

Anyhow, the woman told her that she was well connected, and could bring her a lot of business. Again, I'd heard this story hundreds, if not thousands, of times. It is a common story that people will tell you to bring your anointing and your business under subjection to them. These people are what I call anointing vampires, and they will use whomever they can to get what they want. They are often great talkers who have a lot of knowledge and energy, but no real connections. I described this woman's ways to her, and she was amazed because I didn't know the woman. It wasn't prophecy; it was discernment. I had dealt with that spirit before, so I knew what she'd say, what she'd do, and how she'd react when the girl attempted to disassociate herself from her.

There are many types of opposition that you will face, but having your own business is worth it all, because even in the secular workplace, you will face opposition. At least in your own business, you can control your environment and send opposition away from you. For example, any time I get a customer who is puffed up and tries to talk down on me, I refuse to take their order. If they've paid me, I refund them. If they haven't paid me, I'll sometimes look for another company to send them to. Now, in the secular world of entrepreneurship, this would be a bad business move because they are taught that the customer is always right. In the Christian realm of things, holding on to bad customers can literally drain the life out of your business because your opposition is often spiritual.

In addition, there are some legal risks involved with running a business. My suggestion is to only link your business or organization up to the governmental entities that you must by law link them up to. If not, you will be forced to go against what you believe in the name of "the people" or better yet, the people of the world. (They don't care what the church thinks since you are a small percentage.)

As a Christian entrepreneur, you are often called to come against your own understanding, and this can be quite the war. You have to prepare your heart to receive the knowledge that GOD avails you through this new journey of yours. Expect to be challenged by others and by your own misunderstandings occasionally. More than that, learn to overcome the opinions of others and to embrace a whole new way of thinking. You will only be as successful as you believe you can be. This means that if your vision is obstructed by your lack of faith or knowledge, you need to get your heart cleaned up so that your vision can be clearer.

It's your business, and how you mind it will determine how it minds you.

The Mind To Succeed

A mind to succeed only comes from the LORD; therefore, it has to be prayed in and believed for. *"Faith comes by hearing and hearing by the WORD of GOD (Romans 10:17)."* Just as faith comes in through our praying and learning the WORD, fear has to be run out through activation of the WORD in our lives.

GOD gives gifts, but just like those gifts our parents used to give us, our GOD-given gifts have to be opened. We have to perform the works to display the evidence of our faith in HIM. You will come across many who have gifts, but they don't use them because they either don't realize that they are there, don't like having them, or they are intimidated by another person with that very same gift. They keep comparing their gifts to the gifts of others and letting fear intimidate them to silence.

Once you have asked and believed GOD for this mindset, you must continue to search the scriptures to have those old ways of thinking evicted from your heart. This is a process, so you will have to be patient; not just with GOD, but with your own self. Oftentimes, the LORD will immediately open the doors to begin our journeys, but our lack of knowledge, lack of faith, and abundance of fear often keeps us from walking through them. Fear and lack of faith blinds the man from seeing those doors, but believing in one's own failures opens the natural eyes to see one's own manifested realities. These realities don't speak to GOD'S inability to do as HE has promised, for GOD is faithful, and HIS WORD will not and has never returned to HIM void. These realities, however, do mirror our faith or lack thereof, so rather than constantly praying for success or whatever you are praying for, sometimes you just need to pray for more faith and study the WORD for more faith. Too many times, people ask the LORD for something over and over again, but they never see the manifestation of what they have been praying for. After this, they conclude that believing GOD is fruitless, but in truth, the error was and is never found in GOD; it was found in their less than a mustard-seed sized faith.

Oftentimes, people just pray the wrong prayers and neglect to take the right steps. Their lives will always reflect what they believe.
One of the keys to success is having an unwillingness to fail. It is having a determination that is unyielding, no matter what serves itself as your reality today. A mind to succeed is not considering failure as an option or quitting as an alternative. A mind to succeed is what it says it is; a heart of faith and the will to go with it. Success will always start in the mind first and then begin to manifest outwardly. Someone with the mind to succeed does not see a seemingly failing business as a bad investment. They don't change the business or career that they are in; they change their approach to what they've been doing, whereas someone who hasn't tapped into this level of faith will just jump around from one profession to the next. They never even allow themselves to get to the level of expert or professional; instead, they usually change careers while they are still in the rookie stage. What you are witnessing with this character is a lack of faith and a lack of patience; therefore, they remain a rookie at everything. If there was a career that one could jump right into and immediately find success, most of America would be in it. It's not that simple because, again,

success first starts in the mind or better yet, the heart before it begins to make its way to the outside. Your mind will be pregnant with success and eventually give birth to it when you let the seasons run their course, but fear will always abort success and impatience will always cause you to miscarry success. This is why you absolutely have to stay in the faith lane and refuse to take detours and exits that promise to get you to where you want to be quicker.

The right kind of friends will always support and encourage you to pursue the LORD and all that HE has for you. In addition, they will be pursuing the LORD and all that HE has for them. If they are not, they've stopped their vehicle and will always ask or demand that you stop yours at some point so that you don't take off and leave them behind. The wrong kind of friends may project a false sense of support, but with eyes wide open, you should be able to see through their facade. Real support shows its evidence, whereas non-existent support is as void as the joy in their voice.

The world teaches you to surround yourself with like-minded individuals, but this is good when you arrive at your "cruise-control" height and you don't plan on going up anytime soon. However, when you are growing, you need to surround yourself with people that are where you want to be. They aren't necessarily like-minded because their goals and your goals may be different or their approach may be different from yours. Their way of thinking will, more than likely, be foreign to you. Don't aspire to attain their success, but it is always better to aspire to be all that you can be in CHRIST JESUS. When looking at the success of others, you may be so distracted by what looks like success that you end up tapping into their failures. Some people just know how to look successful, but they are critically in debt, and their businesses are on life support. They won't tell you this, however, because they may see an opportunity in you to resuscitate their business. This is because you, at the time, may be naïve to the way that type of business operates, but full of the zeal and the faith they need to breathe life back into their business. Let them be an inspiration, but not an aspiration. Inspire to be more successful than you believe them to be, but aspire to be who you see yourself as in JESUS CHRIST. Sometimes people can and will be that fuel you need to get you a few more miles closer to who you are, but it is always an error to follow up behind who they are, who they think they are, or who they pretend to be. Sometimes you're so busy chasing their dreams that you don't even realize they are chasing someone else's dreams. As a result, you find yourself on this highway to nowhere, pressing the pedal to the metal and running out of fuel. When they are finally burned out and you pass them, you think you're going somewhere, but you're on a highway that GOD built for someone else. That highway may be long and wide for you, and you'll pass other lost souls along the way, but eventually you'll find yourself further away from who you really are, trying to find your way back to you. Why prolong your arrival at your blessed place tailgating someone else to nowhere?

To change your mind, you have to change the information that goes into your mind. This means that you have to change the people around you that are feeding you this information, and you need to search out the information that you'll need to start your journey. It's not easy to convince the mind to change. This is actually where you'll fight your greatest battle against yourself. You have to command the mind to change by subjecting it to new information. During this process, you may find yourself getting drowsy when you attempt to study, or you may find yourself easily distracted by imaginations when you attempt to study. This is when and where you need to take a stand against the opposing forces that are coming against your destiny. Who are these opposing forces? The enemy and your flesh. Whenever you find yourself struggling to get into studying or working, this is the time when you have to actively and consciously study harder and work harder. You need to decree and declare some things into the atmosphere and bind up anything that opposes GOD'S will for you.

To change your mind, you have to present yourself as a living sacrifice, holy and acceptable unto GOD. This means that you have to sacrifice the selfish and sinful desires of self to embrace the will of GOD. Self may want to go and take a nap, but your business may need you to put some time into it. Sometimes, what you need to do is simply take a break to collect yourself, and if a nap is absolutely needed, take one. If you can fight it off, do so. We often become drowsy about an hour or two after eating. For me, when this onset of drowsiness starts, I'll usually begin making calls to my clients or advertising. Sometimes, I'll return a friend's call and do that portion of work that doesn't require my undivided attention. Eventually, that drowsiness wears off and I'm able to get back to work.

The mind to succeed is focused and unyielding. There will be times when someone says to you that you're putting too much time, effort, and money into your business. You have to remember that in CHRIST, you are super-ordinary which means that ordinary people may not understand your vision, views, or drive. We serve a peculiar GOD, and the more we walk in obedience, the more we become like our FATHER. This renders us peculiar and separates us from the world.

The mind to succeed is unapologetic. Your drive will intimidate many, especially if they are in business for themselves and can't understand your dedication to your craft. Your success will offend many, but they are not really offended with or by you; they are angered by the fact that they believe they deserve this success more than you do. In many cases, I have found Christians constantly apologizing for being blessed. Sure, they don't outright say, "Hey, I'm sorry that I'm blessed. Please forgive me." But, in most cases, someone may apologize for mentioning their success or try to downplay their success to keep from offending someone who isn't successful. If you can't be as blessed as GOD made you to be around the people that you know, it's time to get away from them. You are who you are, and in CHRIST, you will continue to find out more about your identity in HIM. You will open up more gifts, and you will change more to fit into the anointing that GOD has designed for you. It's not so much that you are changing from being one person into another, but you are changing back into who you are. The real you got lost some time ago or was suppressed by hardships, but as Satan's lies and fear fall away from you, you will begin to emerge as the real you. The average person constantly apologizes for this change. The average person reaches back into the familiar and back into their hurt places to continue to identify with the people that they know. The average person doesn't do well because they didn't realize that, to own a blooming and successful business, they would have to be more than average. People may say things like, "Yeah, I earned a lot of money on Labor Day weekend, but you know how that is. I earned it only to have to pay it back out on bills. It's hard out there." That statement is to keep the listener from being offended and keep the listener believing that the speaker can relate to their hardships. Again, if you've got to monitor what you say, then why continue in that friendship? If you've got to murmur and complain to fit in, it's because you are in a relationship that is not a good fit for you.

A mind to succeed does not dance around with doubt. Sure, the music may be playing and lack may be crouching at the doorway of your business, but it doesn't mean that you have to dance your way to the door and let it in. Instead, this is a great opportunity to glorify GOD by showing off your staying power and your faith. Your situation may say to you that you have failed, but it is up to you whether you accept this report or accept GOD'S report. Whatever you believe, you will receive.

A mind to succeed is already successfully believing GOD for every good thing and believing that GOD will block every bad thing. A mind to succeed ties its dreams up to the WORD of GOD and waits with expectation for the season of harvest to arrive.

You have to constantly challenge your mind and feed your mind. A mind to succeed doesn't change just because it is met with obstacles, but it uses those obstacles as opportunities to prove its determination and GOD'S strength.

What if you don't have this kind of mind? Well, it's just a prayer and a few works away. It is easy to retreat back to what you know, but it is better to pursue what you don't know. Set a schedule for yourself and refuse to break it. There will be times when you want to just have a day off, and it's okay to take them when you absolutely need them, but please know the difference between laziness and tiredness. Pay attention to the dedication of someone that is sculpting their body. They eat certain foods, exercise at certain times of the day, and so on. In the beginning, it was hard for them because they had to give up the familiar pleasures of what they'd grown to love to embrace something strange, and oftentimes tasteless. They had to absolutely change their mind before they could take on this journey. You will find them dedicated to sculpting their bodies, to the point where you may wonder what is driving them. Passion is driving them. They have become so dedicated to the cause that they are consistent with their schedules. They see ordinary people and wonder why they allow themselves to pick up unhealthy weight. This is a changed mind and the power therein.

According to studies, it takes 17-21 consecutive days to form or break a habit. Try scheduling yourself for a month to study the WORD, learn your craft and make certain achievements in your business. Don't set easy goals for yourself or you may become lax. Instead, set goals that challenge you, but don't overwhelm you. Set realistic goals that require research, dedication, and sacrifice. Set unrealistic goals that require faith. You are challenging yourself, and these challenges will cause you to find the strength that GOD has placed in you. At the same time, these challenges will give you an opportunity to see GOD at work. Rather than setting a 21-day schedule, try setting a 31-day schedule and absolutely refuse to break one day. Keep your schedule consistent and be sure to make enough moves in a day to cause you to feel that you have accomplished something that day. You should see obvious progressions in your business each day, even if they are minor. Make it a point to accomplish something every day. For me, I won't go to bed until I have completed a task each and every day. They don't have to be major tasks, but I try to complete a task each day so the next day, I won't have to continue working on tasks from the previous day. Instead, I'm able to start and complete a few new tasks and get closer to the finished mark. This is why I tend to finish projects a lot faster than most.

If you're serious about taking and successfully completing this journey, you will be required to make some sacrifices, but it's all worth it. The journey isn't purposed in killing you, but it does show you different shades of you until you find your true match.

<u>Your Gift Or Their Gift</u>

This chapter is one that you need to pay special attention to. Not that all of what is written here isn't important, because it is, but this chapter will serve as an eye opener for many. It's time to be conscious about who you are and who you are pretending to be.

Most people that launch businesses don't launch from their own gifting; they attempt to claim the dreams, visions, and gifts of someone else as their own. This is common because of the infamous quadruplets: impatience, lack of faith, an unwillingness to find and tap into the gifts that GOD has given them, and an unwillingness to obey GOD.

You will come in contact with many Christians that have successful businesses, but it doesn't mean that the market they are in is a goldmine; it could simply mean that they are anointed to do what they are doing. Nevertheless, most aspiring business owners don't see it that way. Instead, they see dollar signs and they pursue the wealth with vigor. Before you know it, they're launching themselves out in the gifts of another person and trying to find their footing in someone else's gifts. The problem is, this isn't their calling, so they won't do well in it. They may get a few sales, but eventually they have to find their way back to the starting point of who they really are.

For me, getting the news that someone that I know is tapping into another marketing avenue is not a surprise anymore because I mentor people about launching their own Christian businesses. What is a surprise is when they tell me why they want to launch into the particular field they chose. Usually, they ran into someone that was doing well in that field, and they discovered that they too could do what that person is doing. Then it comes. They start paying hundreds and thousands for branding, spending excessive amounts of time on marketing, and calling me up trying to get some pointers; which, by the way, aren't free. After they are set up, they begin looking for customers. Why aren't they getting the success that the other person has garnered? This is a common question. They spend weeks, months, and sometimes years trying to fit into another person's gifting, but it doesn't work. Eventually, they angrily head back to the drawing board, vowing not to speak to their friends and family anymore because they didn't support them or their business.

The problem here isn't a lack of patience, since some of them have that. (Sadly enough, people tend to have more patience trying to fit into someone else's shoes than they do trying to walk in their own.) The problem is they tried to fit into an anointing that was too big or too small for them. Many don't see or recognize their own errors in this, so they go on to blame others for the failure of their business. Trying to help them to see the truth is like trying to pet an alligator with a pork-chop, and trying to get them to accept the truth is like trying to tickle a rattlesnake. Sometimes you just have to let the truth strike people or roll them around before they'll pay attention to where they are putting their hands.

Let's say you're here because you want to start your own

business. That's great; congratulations! Are you launching from the bag of blessings that GOD has given you, or are you launching from a bag belonging to someone else? The easier way to answer this is to ask yourself about your own motive for launching out. When GOD gives you a gift, you will find that you are passionate about it and you want to share it with the nations. You simply love what you are doing, and the bonus is you can get paid for sharing this information. That's when you know that you are reaching into your own bag. But when it is not your gifting, you won't be passionate about it, and your motive will almost always be to obtain the wealth, prestige, and notoriety of someone else. What have you been envisioning? You may find yourself envisioning greatness, big houses, and lots of fans. This is your heart showing you the motive that is residing in it. If your motives are pure, you may find yourself imagining more opportunities to share the wealth of information that is in you, and this will be more exciting than the thought of financial gain. Financial gain is just a bonus for a person who is gifted to do what they are doing. Financial gain is the driving factor behind someone who is not gifted to do what they are doing, but they are skilled enough to do it. This means they are hunting money. This, of course, is a perverted way of thinking, since we are always supposed to be pursuing the Truth and how we can please HIM. Perverted means you are heading in the wrong direction, being led by selfish desires.

If you have found that you are chasing money; it's not too late to turn back around and pursue GOD'S will for your life. Even if you have invested thousands of dollars and thousands of hours into your skill, it is better to get back on the right path now and begin your journey than it is to continue on the wrong path and arrive at nowhere. Simply pray about your walk and don't be afraid of what GOD reveals to you. Be willing to turn around if HE shows you that you are in fact in hot pursuit of wealth.

"A man's gift maketh room for him, and bringeth him before great men" (Proverbs 18:16). We all know that an apostrophe is used to show ownership. In the scripture here, the word

"man's" is a possessive noun. It is basically saying that the word "gift" is in possession by the noun that precedes it. This is to say that a man's own gift will make room for him. A woman's own gift will make room for her. Your gift will make room for you. Sally's gift won't make room for Sue. Sure, people have been known to launch out into something they are obviously not called to and find financial success, but success cannot be dismembered into parts. Success is whole or it is non-existent. This is why you will find that many people who have acquired financial wealth aren't anywhere near the gates of happiness. They didn't realize that they were sacrificing happiness for financial gain or notoriety. Like many in poverty, they are addicted to drugs, addicted to alcohol, and surrounded by people who only love their money. These people aren't successful; they are wealthy failures. It is sad that most people alive believe that money will make them happy, when in truth, money will only bring in a whole slew of issues that you aren't wise enough to deal with. GOD has to ready you for financial wealth by giving you spiritual wealth. Without the spiritual wealth of wisdom, financial success will always put you in harm's way. It'll isolate you from love and surround you with misguided souls that think that wealth is the key to happiness. So you'll have to stay on guard at all times.

Your gift will make room for you. The key is to find out what your gifts are and how to tap into them. How do you discover what your gifting is? What is in you oftentimes makes its way to the surface, even when you were a sinner, but you didn't recognize it. It was your gifting. For example, one of my talents is design. I've always been passionate about design, and I've always liked that rich Kingdom look. So, in elementary school, I made me a few skirts to wear to school. They weren't the sturdiest, but they did last through a few wearings. I also started drawing in kindergarten. I loved to draw people. In middle school, I found that I loved to write, and I would write books on notebook paper and share them with my class. In high school, I developed a love for artistic, colorful eye shadowing. As a young adult, I started making gift baskets and eventually, when I moved into my first house, I found that I had a passion for interior design and then poetry. These were already instilled in me by GOD, but only in obedience was I able to perfect the gifts and open up more of my gifts.

It works the same way with you. There is more than likely something that you have always loved to do, and maybe it flew under the radar. Maybe you are a great singer or maybe you have always been excessively talkative (like me). Talkative people are often gifted to write, minister, or counsel others. When a person is perverted, they misuse their gifts and promote the kingdom of darkness. It's very common to see someone who is anointed to worship the LORD in song singing for the world. What and who you are is already a part of you, but obedience to GOD will often unlock the tools that you'll need to fully utilize the gifts that you have. The gifts don't go away just because one is a sinner, for Romans 11:29 reads: *"For the gifts and calling of God are without repentance."* GOD will let you choose how you use the gifts that HE has given you, but if your gifts aren't glorifying HIM, you may find yourself on the other end of HIS wrath. Matthew 25:14-30 reads: *"For the kingdom of heaven is as a man traveling into a far country, who called his own servants, and delivered unto them his goods. And unto one he gave five talents, to another two, and to another one; to every man according to his several ability; and straightway took his journey. Then he that had received the five talents went and traded with the same, and made them other five talents. And likewise he that had received two, he also gained other two. But he that had received one went and digged in the earth, and hid his lord's money.*
After a long time the lord of those servants cometh, and reckoneth with them. And so he that had received five talents came and brought other five talents, saying, Lord, thou deliveredst unto me five talents: behold, I have gained beside them five talents more. His lord said unto him, Well done, thou good *and* faithful servant*: thou hast been faithful over a few things, **I will make thee ruler over many things: enter thou into the joy of thy lord.***

*He also that had received two talents came and said, Lord, thou deliveredst unto me two talents: behold, I have gained two other talents beside them. His lord said unto him, Well done, good and faithful servant; thou hast been faithful over a few things, **I will make thee ruler over many things: enter thou into the joy of thy lord.***

Then he which had received the one talent came and said, Lord, I knew thee that thou art an hard man, reaping where thou hast not sown, and gathering where thou hast not strawed: And I was afraid, and went and hid thy talent in the earth: lo, there thou hast that is thine.

*His lord answered and said unto him, Thou wicked and **slothful servant**, thou knewest that I reap where I sowed not, and gather where I have not strawed: Thou oughtest therefore to have put my money to the exchangers, and then at my coming I should have received mine own with usury. **Take therefore the talent from him, and give it unto him which hath ten talents.***

***For unto every one that hath shall be given, and he shall have abundance: but from him that hath not shall be taken away even that which he hath.** And cast ye the unprofitable servant into outer darkness: there shall be weeping and gnashing of teeth."*

The whole scripture is important, but I wanted to bring attention to a few of the statements made. As you can see, I underlined "good" and "faithful." We all know what good means. It means that we are like our FATHER, for HE is good and HIS mercy endures forever. Faithful means loyally consistent without pause. Again, GOD is faithful because HE changes not. Therefore, the servants that were called "good" and "faithful" were being made aware that they were in right-standing with their Master. They were doing the will of their Master and he was pleased. As a result, he said that he would make them ruler over many things. This implies promotion, elevation, and a higher ranking. When you and me are in the will of GOD, HE will always promote us and bless us with more. Don't forget, however, that to whom much is given, much is required. This is often forgotten by believers that have been promoted to rankings of greatness and notoriety. In right-standing, more gifts will begin to manifest, and promotion is always on the scene.

Then, there was the servant who was called "wicked" and "slothful." There was a reason that his Master only gave him one talent. It was because he couldn't be trusted. He wasn't a faithful servant, nor was he a righteous servant. He only did what he felt was expected of him and nothing more. He was left with a talent, and he did nothing with it. He was wicked because he did not do the will of his Master. His words even demonstrated that he had ill-feelings towards his Master. He didn't love him. Instead, he tolerated him and did as he was told. How many Christians are doing this today? You'd be amazed at the amount of souls that do not love HIM, but they tolerate HIM, hoping to get to the blessings of GOD. In other words, they try to use HIM.

He was called slothful because he was obviously lazy. He didn't want to do the work needed to add onto that talent. Instead, he chose to bury it so that he could give it back to the Master when he returned. Most of the people alive today that have talents have buried their talents. They simply do not want to do anything with those talents because it requires work. So they bury them, and they'll return to the dirt, having done nothing with the talent. A talent is given to glorify GOD. A talent is never given to just be parked in a person.

The LORD then required that the talent that the wicked servant had be taken from him and given to the faithful servant who now had ten talents. Did you know that in your faithful serving of the LORD through your obedience that you'd be blessed with the talents that other folks aren't using? Because GOD can trust you with that talent to glorify HIS Name. Can you imagine having been born with ten talents and having those talents doubled due to your faithfulness? Then having those now twenty talents doubled because of your faithfulness, then forty and so on? The goal isn't to just be alive, but the aim is to be successfully alive. This means to accomplish that in which you were put here to do. That is success! It's not hidden from you; you've just got to be willing to see it.

"Enter now into the joy of the LORD." Do you know the value of entering into the joy of the LORD? People spend too much time chasing money and material things, and they get so far away from the joy of the LORD that they live in rich depression. The joy of the LORD is peace and a joy from within. It is having a sound mind and not a worry to your name. I would rather be poor and have the joy of the LORD than to be rich and not have it. If you haven't learned to appreciate your sanity, go into a psych ward and see what these people are living with. Many of them are in there because they chased the wrong things and the wrong people down dark roads and into the realms of the demonic. While you may stand in the same room with them, your mind is in a completely different place than theirs.

The last statement, *"for unto every one that hath shall be given, and he shall have abundance: but from him that hath not shall be taken away even that which he hath"* is pretty self explanatory. It says that for everyone that has, more will be given, but for everyone that does not have, even what they possess will be taken away. If you read this statement wrong, you'll think that GOD isn't being fair, but think about why someone has something and why someone doesn't have it. They have because they chose to follow the LORD, and those that don't have are lacking because they chose to turn away from the LORD. For those that have, they are faithful, and GOD knows that HE can trust them with what HE has given them; that's why HE gave it to them. For those that are lacking, they are unfaithful, and GOD knows that they can't be trusted; that's why HE takes away even what they have. Look at the walk of the Israelites, after they finally accomplished their punishment of 40 years in the wilderness. They went to war and killed millions of people and took their lands. In modern day, we'd say that this was wrong. In reading the book of Deuteronomy and the book of Joshua, you will find that GOD was telling them to go up to war and possess the land. HE often told them to leave no one alive. Sometimes they were allowed to plunder the wealth of the place, and other times they were not. Why did GOD allow them to kill all of these people? Because the earth is the LORD'S and the fullness thereof. *(See Psalms 24:1)* The people that GOD allowed Israel to slaughter were not serving HIM. They were worshiping other gods in the earth that belongs to HIM! Can you imagine someone living in your house and paying rent to your enemy? Israel belongs to GOD so HE kept adding lands, territories, and wealth to them; but for those nations that did not serve HIM, HE took whatever they had. They could speak; yet they chose not to glorify HIM. They could walk; yet they chose not to follow HIM. They could build; yet they chose to build up altars for devils. They knew of HIM; yet they chose not to know HIM. The ability to walk, talk, and breathe is a gift in itself! When we use it to sin, death comes along and takes those abilities away.

You are gifted, I'm sure, but where are your gifts and what are your gifts? Are you tapping into your gifts or the gifts of someone else? When you tap into your own; you are worshiping GOD, but when you tap into what is not yours; you are trusting in yourself. Get on your knees and pray for GOD to show you your gifts and to give you the faith, obedience, and faithfulness needed to glorify HIM with all that you do. After all, owning a Christian business is not all about you. It should be always purposed in glorifying GOD in every way possible. Sure, you want to leave an inheritance for your children and your children's children, but this will only be done if you are what GOD refers to as a "good" man. A good man is a righteous man or woman. This is someone that is in HIS will and doing HIS will on purpose. On purpose implies what you have willed yourself to do, whereas HIS purpose for you implies what you were created to do. When the two meet up and agree, you will discover your gifts and just how powerful they are. You will then be willing to do what HE created you to do. Activate your gifts today by getting in HIS will. There is no better or safer place to be. In HIS will, you will never have to try to figure out who you are and how you will survive because HE will supply you with the knowledge that you need to know you and know HIM.

<u>Doing Business As A Minority</u>

Before starting my business, I never considered the challenges that I would face because of my race, gender, and my Christianity. Even if I had taken these things into consideration, I never would have believed that the challenges that presented themselves would be mostly delivered to me from people that were like me: African American and Christian. I can't say that I've been challenged more by women than men, but I can say I was challenged in different ways by both women and men alike.

First off, being African American or a minority already places your business in a sub-category, and you will have to fight to rise above that category. The great thing about America, however, is that it doesn't have to stay in that category, but you can rise to have a large and profitable company.

I used to hear African American business owners complaining about other African Americans and, at first, I didn't get it. The general complaint is colorful manipulation. That is when someone uses the fact that your skin is the same as theirs, and they try to play the "sister" or "brother" card to get their service or product discounted or freely. I have come in contact with quite a few manipulative characters that did try to play the race card, but they are rare. They aren't the majority. One of the more common manipulations that I have found, however, was people using the fact that the business owner is Christian, and they'll try to play on that to get a free service or a discount.

When I first started doing business, I became somewhat bitter because I was coming in contact with so many manipulative characters who tried to play on my gender or my Christianity. What infuriated me the most was that these characters were Christian or allegedly Christian. Someone would try to deal personally with me by telling me their stories or testimonies, and then follow it up with a hint that they had little to no income. Some would play around for a while and wait to see if I would offer a free service or a discount, and when that didn't happen, they'd ask me upfront. Then, there were the patient ones who called again and again trying to establish some kind of "cliendship" (that's what I call a client posing as a friend). They would use hinting, pity, and all types of wiles trying to get free services. I even got quite a few attempts of prophesying from others who happened to want a service. I remember one particular week, I'd gotten around three people who said they were prophesying to me, and immediately after they finished, they asked the very same question: "Also, I need a seal/ logo. How much are you going to charge me?" This was because I wasn't mature as a business owner at that time. Once or twice, I must admit, I fell for it. As I began to mature and recognize this as witchcraft (the false ones anyway), I learned how to deal with such characters, and I will share this information with you later in this chapter.

Lastly, as a woman, I found that some men were somewhat flirtatious, even though they claimed to be Christian and they knew that I was married; but this is very rare. As a business owner, you have to be aware of the devices out there that people will use to get over on you. With women, I found a few to be condescending, prideful, and competitive. Now, this is not with all women because most of my female customers are great, anointed, and loving women of GOD; but I have dealt with the wrong kind of women as well. After a while, you'll be able to immediately pick up on their spirit, and know how or if you want to do business with them. For me, I send condescending customers away because they are power-thirsty, time-consuming and energy-draining. Don't get me wrong, I have come in contact with men that were like this as well, but the majority of the time when I have dealt with a rude customer, it was a woman. I believe that in businesses run by males, the results may be opposite. A man may find that most of their challenging, condescending, and competitive customers are male; whereas a woman will find these behaviors in other women. Personally, I believe those behaviors started when they were in the world. During that time, they learned to deal with the opposite sex and the same sex in a certain way, and many have never been delivered from those ways of thinking. It doesn't mean that they aren't real Christians; sometimes it simply means that this is an area where they haven't grown up yet. For example, many women see men as superior beings and treat them as such; whereas they see women as objects of competition and behave in catty manners towards them. Many men see women as inferior, emotional creatures, and they will appeal to a woman's emotions when doing business with her; whereas they see other men as potential friends or challengers, and they'll attempt to relate to them or challenge them.

But, let's go beyond that and talk about how you can protect your business. Review and apply the tips below:
1. Do not prejudge. One of the worst things you can do is try to pre-think how a person is going to act. This will only cause you to act offensively in an attempt to protect your business from your perceived threat. I did this at one point. I had come across so many rude women customers that I would prepare myself whenever a woman attempted to make an order. Of course, I prayed my way out of this thinking and found that not having rules set in place was the reason I'd met so many challenging customers. After I set, applied, and abode by my

own rules, I found that most of my female clientele are really kind and beautiful souls to know. The ones that were problematic were just stretching themselves out where there were no rules in place, so it was my own fault. Prejudging will only cost you business and rob you from seeing the other side of things. Someone that prejudges always pays attention to the negatives that confirm what they think, and they ignore the positives that show otherwise.

2. Beware of the "sister" and "brother" talks if you are a minority. Now, some people in the Christian realm refer to one another as sister or brother, but you will always be able to discern how they are using it after you've been in business for a while. Many people (like myself) refer to other Christians as sister or brother, but when someone is telling you a pity story, followed by those endearing terms, oftentimes they are trying to manipulate you. Not always, but most times. It is always great to have rules in place that keep you protected from such types. For example, let's say that you had a marketing agency, and someone comes along that needs marketing. They go on to tell you about how hard times have been, the rough patches that they are getting over, having dealt with a recent death in the family, and the prayers that they've been sending up for help. You will feel and learn to recognize that emotional "pull" on your wallet. The right thing to do is to show empathy, tell them that you will lift them up in prayer, and immediately refer them to your website to show them the plans available. You do not want to share your personal life story with them (unless GOD tells you to do so) because they are trying to identify with you on a personal level, whereas you are trying to run a business. If you get personal with them, they won't place an order, but instead, they'll continue to call you again and again with pity stories. Their goal is to get a free service, product, or a discount. It may sound cruel to have to redirect their conversation to the website, but after dealing with this type of character for a few years, you'll learn that this is a common tactic that people use to manipulate others.

3. Set rules about random prayers and prophesies. Now, if the LORD is speaking, I want to hear HIM. That's a given, but many

times, people will "prophelie". I have a rule that instructs my clients and potential clients that I do not allow for prayer attempts. This is because everyone does not belong to GOD, and you don't always know who they are praying to. Prayer often opens doors into your life that you would have to pray closed. I have had a few people that have asked if they could pray for me, and I politely declined. Then, there are the ones who will suddenly start praying for you, and in these instances, you have to decide what you want to do. You can speak up, or you can begin a silent prayer, covering yourself, family, spouse, and ministry with the Blood of JESUS. After they complete the prayer (if you're still on the line), you can inform them of your rule. As far as prophecies, it's kind of hard to set rules in relation to that, because they usually come all of a sudden. But if you feel GOD in it, definitely welcome it. If you don't feel HIM, and you feel that it is out of order and rooted in witchcraft, you can politely cut them off or just pray. These are weird rules, but this is what happens when you have a Christian business and your clientele is primarily Christian.

4. Absolutely, without a question, don't allow someone to swear or use obscene language in your business or in your ear. Whatever you allow will become commonplace, and if you plan for your business to be around for a while, it is always good to consider everyone who will do business with you. Now, I haven't had anyone swear in my ear (thank GOD), but depending on the type of business that you are or will be running, you have to set rules accordingly.

5. Another common form of manipulation that I've come in contact with is when someone attempts to get you to join their church or come on their prayer line. Sometimes people are just trying to be nice, and then there are the ones who are trying to stir you up emotionally so they don't have to deal with you professionally. They want to deal with you personally because you are gifted. It's as simple as that. Your gift will draw many to you, and they won't want to just do business with you; they'll want more. You have to enforce the rules to prevent these types of attachments. I had a girl call me once, and she said that she needed a logo. Anyhow, she then started trying to get

me to come onto her prayer line. I declined, of course and after that, she called me a couple of times still trying to get me to come onto her prayer line. When that didn't work, I never heard from her again, and she never placed the order. Why did she do this? Because she was trying to stir me up emotionally to condition me to sow into her.

6. Keep it professional and stay away from personal-business relationships, because you're going to eventually have to choose between the two. I made the mistake of befriending one of my clients. Everything was a-okay until she needed a service, and I quoted her the price. This was offensive to her because she felt like since we were now friends, and I knew her personal struggles, I was being a horrible friend by charging her for a service. After all, here I am married and both of us are working, but she was a single woman with no job. How horrible was I? When I was her graphic designer alone, there were no problems and she paid without pause. Her economic situation didn't come into play then. When I became her friend, she wanted to deal with me only as a friend. When I tried to go back to the business side of things, she took offense. She went on to disassociate from me and delete me on social networking sites because I tried to charge her for a service. The error was not in her; it was in me. If you intend to do business with people, keep it professional. Once someone sees you as a friend, they will automatically place their friendship demands (yokes) on you, and when you don't honor them, you'll lose them as a friend. The minute you started dealing with them personally, you lost them as a client because in many cases, they will not want to pay you, or they will expect discounts. Sure, there will be many super-nice clients that you wouldn't mind talking to and knowing personally, but this is never a good idea unless you've been doing business with them for a long time, and they are mature enough to separate business from friendship in their heads. You'll know if you have the green light or not after they've been a client for a while. Just remain prayerful. (Now, some of my clients I do talk to occasionally, but we've been doing business for years, and they understand that they have to pay for a service. In

addition, we only talk when they are ordering a service.)

7. Don't make rules that target your challenging customers only. When you first start off in business, you will get a few headaches in dealings with your clients. This is because you're new and learning, and there are plenty of sharks out there that like to feed on new business owners. With no rules in place, the customer will stretch you as far as they can. After being stretched out of place a few times, you may find yourself hastily and angrily typing up a set of rules to protect yourself from future problems. You have to think as the client and not as the owner. What if you went to a website and you were reviewing the rules and they sounded rude and there were no positive rules listed? You'd escape from that place, more than likely because your perception of this business is now a negative one. It is always good to write rules that benefit the customers and mix them with the rules that protect your business and the customer. Let's say you do a f.a.q. (frequently asked questions) page in place of a rules and guidelines page. You're thinking about the last few customers that tried to get over on you, so your f.a.q.s look like this:

Question: How much is a window washing?

Answer: As posted on the website, window washing starts at $39.99.

Question: I have three vehicles and I wanted to get them all detailed. Are there any discounts available for people with multiple vehicles?

Answer: No. The prices are as posted on our website.

Question: Free Willie's Car Detail is offering a sale for a full detail for $69.99. Do you honor competitive ads?

Answer: As stated in questions 1 and 2, our prices are as posted on the website.

Do you see how this could steer someone away from your site? Your frustration can be felt. Instead, review how these question and answers read. Let's ask the same questions, but relay the answers in a more positive manner.

Question: How much is a window washing?

Answer: Our window washing services start at $39.99.

Question: I have three vehicles and I wanted to get them all detailed. Are there any discounts available for people with multiple vehicles?

Answer: Currently, we don't offer discounts for multiple orders.

Question: My backseat was soiled by my dog. Can you help?

Answer: We can definitely help you! We specialize in detailed cleaning, and our top of the line tools help us to provide a deeper clean than most traditional detailing companies.

Question: Free Willie's Car Detail is offering a sale for a full detail for $69.99. Do you honor competitive ads?

Answer: Currently, we don't honor competitive ads, but we do encourage you to research our F-09 steam washer and Free Willie's T-6 cleaner. You will find that we provide a deeper cleaning than traditional detail companies, so we're worth the extra bucks. Hope to see you soon!

Question: My seats are leather, and I'm not sure if you have the right equipment to clean leather seats. In addition, I wanted to ask if you had some kind of protectant that I could put on my seats because they are beginning to crack.

Answer: You've definitely come to the right place! We manually clean leather seats, and we use Gregory's Wax and Sealant as a protective covering on leather seats. Our customers have told us that this protectant has stopped the cracking and restored that new car look to their seats.

Pay attention to what was done here. You'll notice that a couple of "yes" questions were added. If your customer is reading your frequently asked questions and all of your answers are nos, you may lose your customers. It is always good to insert a few questions or rules that end with the customer getting a yes out of you.

In dealings with customers of another race, it is never a good idea to discuss race relations. As a matter of fact, you should never discuss religious beliefs, race, gender, woman's rights, abortion or politics. People usually feel strongly in these areas and will oppose you ferociously. One day you may feel a special connection with one of your customers. Maybe the two of you are discussing the roles of a woman, and they may say that they don't agree with women as leaders. That's their belief and their business, but now your personal feelings are coming to the surface. You ask them why they believe as they do, and they go on to answer you, and their answer further infuriates you. Do you see how this can stir up a problem? Always remain professional with your clients.

If someone expresses an opinion that you don't agree with, just finish the transaction and politely reroute the conversation. Some people like a good debate and will try to engage in one with you. You're not there for that. In your debating with them, another customer may come into your store and hear your personal beliefs. They may not like your views and decide that they too don't want to do business with you anymore, or that combative customer may share your beliefs with others (word of mouth) and cost you a few more clients. If someone asks you your beliefs, politely tell them that your company's policy instructs you to refrain from those types of discussions. Then throw in a joke and try to start a new discussion.

In dealings with religious customers, it is never a good idea to discuss what you believe unless your beliefs are tied in to your services.

As a minority, the best tip that I can give you is to not see yourself as a minority, but see yourself as a successful business owner without color. You have to act and think like a large corporation and always shoot to be larger than the largest. If I wanted to start an online store like Amazon, it would be better for me to offer services that Amazon does not offer. This gives me my own identity and keeps my business from looking like a generic duplicate of Amazon.

One thing the LORD told me was to never let someone treat my business like a small business. It was a struggle to stand firmly as a one-woman show when I got customers that kept pulling on me to do business their way, but I stood my ground. I lost customers as a result, but I gained a lot more than I lost because I came to find that the customers that go away from you are not customers; they are hindrances with a few bucks on hand. But some of your best customers will come forward and become loyal customers when they see that your business is in order, no matter what your race or gender is. The struggle to stay afloat isn't a hard one. The hardest part is the struggle to claim your place as a hard-hitting and professionally established company and not some back-alley lemonade stand.

As a minority, stand your ground just as the large corporations do, and provide the best service that you can. Put your heart into making sure that you go above and beyond your customer's needs. Put your heartstrings away and never ever let someone operate with you in a way that they wouldn't operate with a larger company such as Wal-Mart or Target. If your goal is to have your company become a major player in today's market, then you have to act like a major player. You will never go far by letting someone hold you back.

Remember this: You are to owe no man anything but to love him.

<u>Setting Unrealistic Goals and Achieving Them</u>

Unrealistic goals are goals that seem out of reach and out of the understanding of man. These are goals that you will have to place in your mind's eye and actually imagine them succeeding. Because as human beings, we are often walled in by lack of faith, and we can't see past our fears. Some people can imagine themselves owning a business that pays them enough to maintain their bills, and others imagine themselves owning a business that pays them the wages of a part-time job. Then, there are the super-ordinary souls who do not just imagine owning a successful business, but they believe and know that their businesses will be successful all around. This is the goal; to get to a super-ordinary way of thinking.

Fear is the opposite of faith. You will either believe GOD or you won't. You will either have faith in GOD or fear of circumstance. You can't have them both. The struggle with business ownership is firing fear and changing the locks on your mind, because fear will always come back and resubmit its application. Even once your business has attained the marks of success, fear will tell you to stop there and go no further. Fear acts as an adviser to you, but fear only gives you bad advice.

Instinctively, we all know how to swim. When a newborn is placed in the water, they automatically hold their breath and start kicking. This is something that GOD has placed inside of every human being. Drowning doesn't occur because one can't swim; drowning occurs when fear overwhelms the person and they believe that they can't swim. This is just how powerful fear is. It'll make one believe that they can't do something, and it'll cause them to hate and steer away from whatever it has taught them to fear.

I've met people that were afraid of just about everything that moves. It's funny because when I was younger, I wasn't afraid of anything. I picked up frogs, worms, killed spiders with my hands, and so on. In elementary school, I used to catch grasshoppers and chase the girls out for recess with them because it was funny to me that they were afraid of such a tiny and harmless insect. As I grew older, fear began to set in, and I too became afraid of frogs, worms, spiders, grasshoppers and so on. I saw this one day and decided to pray against the fear. I knew as a child that a grasshopper couldn't hurt me and I knew as an adult that it couldn't hurt me, but my lost of innocence had robbed me of my faith. After praying for the fear to go, my husband and I took a cruise to Jamaica where I held things that I thought I'd never hold. I held an iguana and I held a snake, and there was absolutely no fear there. I tell this story because I want to demonstrate the power of fear and the lies that are behind it. Sure, what we call common-sense (which is really instinctive sense) tells us not to walk upon a wild snake or an iguana and think we can just pick it up and live happily ever after. But what if your family was cornered by a snake, and to get past it, someone was going to have to go up and wrestle with it? Would you volunteer or would fear cause you to settle in your mind that all of you would just be tomorrow's news? The best thing to do is to learn how to handle a snake, especially if you live in a place where snakes are common. No, you don't have to get out and start practicing on wild snakes, but you can go to some places where they handle snakes and get an education about the snake. That way, should something happen that involves a snake, you would know how to survive it instead of being cornered by fear and lack of knowledge. You could even learn this on the internet. Faith is proactive, whereas fear is active.

Most business owners are controlled, walled-in, and led by fear. They believe that they can only do so much, and they stay within the confines of their beliefs. This is what sets up the perimeters of your business's success or failure. Success or failure does not start on the outside, but it starts from within you. It must first be conceived in your mind and then fed by your faith. Eventually, you'll give birth to whatever you believe, and it'll become your reality. Your reality is not necessarily GOD'S truth. Just the same, when Peter walked on water, reality was and is that water isn't solid; therefore, ordinary people can't walk on it. It took a super-ordinary, supernatural faith for Peter to walk on water. When Peter took his eyes off JESUS, fear began to set in, and he began to sink. The same thing happens in our lives as well as our businesses. When we take our eyes off CHRIST, we begin to sink, and our businesses begin to sink. If we don't do as Peter did and call upon the name of the LORD, we'll find ourselves under fear's hands being drowned by fear.

When you are believing GOD for an extraordinary business, you have to know that people won't understand you, and many will fall away from you. This is because you are operating as a peculiar creature, and people fear and hate what they do not understand. This is why many "normal" people consider some of the richest people to be "weird." It's not that the person or people are strange; what's happened is the people are unrecognizable because of their thinking patterns. Their knowledge is different, and their beliefs are different; therefore, their realities are different. Even in dealings with worldly folks, you'll find that when a person reaches a certain height of knowledge, they'll be given a label that indicates that they stand out from the crowd, and that label is "nerd." Nerds are often castaways, not accepted by the "normal" teens because they aren't normal. The world labels what they do not understand, and so does the church. Now, when you have a super-ordinary amount of wisdom, knowledge and understanding; you won't be called a nerd per sé, but you may find yourself largely welcomed or largely shunned. Not to mention, there are a lot of words that people will call you based on their understanding or lack thereof.

Faith is your fear blocker, and you need to wear it at all times. The most important aspect of running a Christian business is to actually be Christian. It is necessary and mandatory for you to believe GOD. In order to believe GOD, you have to know what GOD said, for faith comes by hearing and hearing by the WORD of GOD. *(See Romans 10:17)* This may be hard for some to take in, but you will have to get into your WORD and get to know HIM. You can't run a Christian business and expect success from CHRIST when you don't know HIM. Knowing HIS Name is not the same as intimately knowing HIM. Yes, there are many secular people out with successful Christian businesses, but they don't have success. Again, success cannot be portioned off; it comes as a whole. Whatever GOD gives, HE adds no sorrow to it. External or secular success may manifest itself as financial success, but the person may have had to sell their peace of mind to get it. This isn't success; it's wearing the mask of success, but what's behind that mask isn't as pretty.

To challenge your fear to a duel, you need to pull out the WORD of GOD and set some unrealistic goals for yourself. Pray over your plans and your business, and begin to work towards those goals. Fear will start to fight with you, but the way you slay fear is with the SWORD of the WORD. The WORD of GOD is a doubled-edged sword, so whenever fear makes its way into you, the WORD will cut you as well. Let's just say that you are starting a business, and you want to earn $25,000 your first year and net $100,000 your second year. These goals sound reasonable to you, but this is because you are speaking from within the walls of your understanding and your fears. Try to up the ante. Set your goals to earn $35,000 the first year and $150,000 the second year. Then, you have to do something super-ordinary. Start investing and working as if you're trying to earn $150,000 your first year. If you try to faith an earnings cap of $35,000; you will have to wrestle with fear to pull it in, and you may find yourself slacking. However, if you set your earnings cap at $150,000; your actual target goal won't be so hard to reach.

You've heard it said: *"Write the vision and make it plain."* *(Habakkuk 2:2)* Did you know that businesses with a business plan and a written plan actually garner 50-75% more success than businesses that don't? It's okay to have plans and ideas, but it is better to write them down. This is a great way to battle fear because you are actually making plans for the future. My husband and I love to watch Investigation Discovery. Someone would go missing, and their spouse would claim not to know where they were. Their spouse's guilt became evident when they made statements that displayed that they didn't believe their spouse would ever return. Some would immediately began to move out their missing spouse's possessions, whereas others began whole new relationships as if they knew the spouse would never return. They knew because they'd killed them. They knew that their spouses were dead. What about your faith in GOD that your business will succeed? Do you believe GOD for the success, or have you stopped planning and writing because you know your faith won't be made alive again? So, you head out to bury your dreams and marry your fears.

Purchase yourself three notebooks and give each notebook a title. Let one be your business plans written out, and publish your ultimate goals for your business in the second one. I'm talking about your unrealistic, hard-to-believe goals. In the third notebook, write a note to yourself reminding yourself of

what you are believing GOD for. Encourage yourself in this note and tell yourself to never give up. The note can read, for example, "If you're reading this note, it means that you are considering giving up. I am the half of you that believes, but there is the part of you that wars with me, and I know it's only because you are afraid of what tomorrow will bring. I am asking you with my whole heart to continue on for me and with me down this faith walk. No one ever said that it would be easy, but I do believe that we serve a GOD that can make the impossible possible. Stand as one with me so that we can no longer be divided in our beliefs, and let's keep it going. No matter what, be sure to continue on, because if you should persevere and win this thing, GOD gets the glory and you get the rewards. Say yes to HIM so that HIS Name can and will be glorified in and through you. It doesn't matter what he or she said. They don't know the relationship you have with GOD, but you do. Let's stand as one together, because GOD called us to be one. No more fear; no more doubts. It's time for you to glorify GOD.
Signed, Your Better Half."

Put this notebook up somewhere and pull it down whenever you feel like quitting. After you've read your note, write yourself another note in response, and then write yourself another encouraging note. Sure, this sounds "cuckoo," but it works. Sometimes, you just have to encourage yourself.

If you have any friends or family members in your circle that are saying that you can't find success in what you are doing, you will have to successfully get them out of your circle. One of the hardest things that I have ever had to do was to let people that I love go. It's not about me, and it's not about them; this walk is about GOD. I had to and have to get to where HE has called me to be, and sometimes that means making some pretty hard choices, but HE is worth it all. I'd do it again if I had to. This is the attitude of success. Some people simply cannot come with you, and until you let them go, you won't even breathe in success's heavenly aroma. I feared letting people go because they'd been there for me in hard times and vice-versa. GOD told me that people are sometimes there for you in hard times because they live there. Come out of hard times and dare to smile, and they'll remind you of your struggles to bring you back into the realms of hurt, where they can relate to you. It's not that they are a great friend; sometimes it's as simple as the two of you being in the same place at the same time. When you come out of that hurt, they won't recognize you, and this is why they'll constantly remind you of the hurts that you have endured. This means that you need to be ministering to that soul, and if they have made their bed in their pain, you have to leave them there and follow the LORD. I'd rather be a bad friend in their sight than a bad daughter in GOD'S sight. You going forth just may be what they need to come out of that comfortable place of death that they've made their beds in. Be willing to let go of the wrong people if you want to grab hold of the right things and meet the right people. As a friend, your responsibility is to act as a brother or a sister and tell your friend the way of the LORD, but they have the feet to walk that way and the mind to choose to walk that way. If they choose to reside in fear, pain, and sin; why are you following them around trying to convince them to move into peace with you? You have to win your own soul before you try to win someone else's. If your best friend sat on a railroad track and refused to move as the train was approaching, would you die with them to prove your undying love? If you did, you would not deserve GOD, and you would find yourself cast away from HIM because HE called you to live for HIM, but you chose to die for a man. It's the same in your walk. You have to choose to go forward for GOD and refuse to stay still for a person. That's why so many business owners end up just like the people they hang around; constantly trying to crank up a dead horse. Where GOD has called you to, you won't be able to bring others into. It was a place set up for you, and as long as you keep these people in your life, you won't enter this blessed place. Instead, you'll dance around the outskirts being lost with them. Don't be afraid to let people go! Yes, they'll be offended; yes, they'll be hurt, but you have to do this for GOD. You have to love them enough to release them to HIM. You can either choose to live within the confines of their definition of a friend, or you can choose to live in the freedoms of being GOD'S son or daughter.

When you want GOD to make an extraordinary move in your life, you will have to do things that are extraordinary. I've heard it said that the definition of insanity is doing the same thing again and again and expecting different results. You will have to go within the realms of the unfamiliar. You will have to embrace new ways of thinking. You will have to do things that you ordinarily wouldn't do. You will find yourself around people that you ordinarily wouldn't hang around. This signifies a change taking place in you, and you don't need to feel guilty about growing up in HIM. Stop apologizing for choosing GOD. Put on your fear blockers and go forward!

__Starting With Or Without a Plan__

It's easy to jump-start a business, but it is easier to lose a business or a great business idea due to inactivity, fear, and procrastination. It's up to you; however, whether you set up the business the right way, or if you try to hope your way to success. People that have a plan do much better than those who do not have a plan. People with a plan have their steps carved out for them; all they have to do is move forward one foot at a time. People without a plan have no idea where they are going; they just go wherever the winds blow.

If you don't start with a plan, it is because you're not that serious or you're not convinced that your business will succeed. Starting a business with the "let's see what happens" mindset is the wrong idea. A business that shoots into the arms of success is most likely run by someone who has a business plan. Let's look at it from the marriage point of view. Most failed marriages are the result of one or two people who came into the union with a preconceived idea of what marriage is and is not. When their spouse or spouses did or said what they felt was not right, they slowly inched their way towards divorce court. In most cases, one or both spouses stayed in the marriage for years, hoping that the other spouse would straighten up and be who and what they believed a spouse should be. When that didn't happen, they gave up on the marriage and decided to try life without a spouse or wait for a spouse that was a better fit for them. Even if you marry the worst person alive, it is never always all their fault that the marriage ended. The doom of that marriage began when you married them, because one or both of you were or are not cut out for one another. We try to fit into someone's heart when they have some quality that we want in a spouse, but in that marriage, truth comes over and drowns reality, and people don't like to live with the truth that their spouse is and will never be who they want them to be. GOD already gave them an identity, and their struggle is to get back to who they are, not who we want. Your business works the same way. Most businesses that fail are handled by someone who expected the business to go one way, but it went in the opposite direction. Rather than muscling their way through the long-suffering, they chose to divorce the idea and try to marry a new idea. People with this way of thinking rarely ever start and run a successful business, since everything we go into will have its share of storms, oppositions, and hardships.

Starting with a plan is a great idea, but you have to continue to add on to that plan. When we add on to something, we are growing the vision; but when we take away from something, we are shrinking the vision. It is very normal to start out with a grand idea but begin to chisel away at some of the layers of that idea when we begin to meet hardships. This isn't the way to start or run a business, since hardships are only life's professors sent to teach us how to handle and rise above adversity.

Let's start you up with a plan. Open up your notebook or a word document to begin writing down your plan. Ask yourself the following questions and answer them truthfully:

What are my realistic short-term goals?

What are my unrealistic short-term goals? (Shoot high in faith; not low in fear.)

What are my realistic long-term goals?

What are my unrealistic long-term goals?

How much am I willing to invest in the launch of my business?

How much am I not willing to invest in the launch of my business and why?

How much do I need to earn to comfortably work from home or in my own business full-time?

How much do I want to earn?

Now, list 5 steps that you are going to take today to make your dream a reality. List realistic and unrealistic steps that can be completed today.

Use the following setup below to guide you in your business plan setup.

Days Of The Week	To Be Accomplished	What Was Accomplished	What Was Not Accomplished and Why
Monday			
Tuesday			
Wednesday			
Thursday			
Friday			
Saturday			
Sunday			

The form above is to be filled out daily. It's not easy at first to get the mind to come out of repetition, but it is necessary and will get easier as time progresses. Just ignore the flesh's attempt to return to what it knows.

Immediate Setups That Need To Be Completed

1. Business Name (Research the name you choose using the U.S. Trademark database.)
2. List Business Services and Products
3. Research and Set Prices
4. Research and Set Up Rules
5. Create or Purchase Slogan or Motto
6. Research Laws In Relation To Your Business Type
7. Research Lawsuits Related To Similar Business Types (To avoid common falls.)
8. List 5 Services That Other Companies Like Yours Do Not Offer, But Should Offer
9. Create Business Account (Paypal is a good place to start if your business will be online.)
10. Business Plan
11. Find Resource Websites That You Can Afford
12. Set Weekly, Bi-monthly, and Monthly Budget
13. Begin Branding Setup (Website, logo, press kit, flyers and so on.)
14. Setup Your Office
15. Apply For a Tax Identification Number (www.irs.gov)
16. Pray Over Your Business (Do this first.)
17. Write Mission Statement
18. List All Tools Needed To Start-Up And Run Company
19. Compare and Contrast Any Area Where You Are Undecided
20. Setup Company Phone Number

Common Christian Errors and Misconceptions

No one has to tell you, I'm sure, that common errors and misconceptions will always lead to the doom of a business. Even the greatest idea requires a plan. Please review the list of common errors and misconceptions so that you can avoid them.

Misconception #1: "I'll just start the business now and invest in it as it grows, if it grows. I don't want to spend too much money now and have the business fail." Someone is always willing to take your idea and do it better than you. One of the worst travesties is to see someone else with your business idea doing well. You've worked hard and thought long, and now someone else is reaping the benefits. When I first started out, the LORD laid on my heart to dominate the market, work hard, and don't love sleep. After I began running the company, I found out that there were a couple of people using my business name. What I knew was that GOD gave me the name, and I wasn't going to back away from it just because someone else was using it. Maybe HE gave it to them too.

Maybe they did nothing with it, but HE told me to continue in it and take it by force. How does this happen? Imagine if you had started a restaurant called Panda Express before the popular restaurant Panda Express came into existence. You had a small little building and a few flyers out. Then, here comes the popular Panda Express and they drown your business into early retirement. What they did was take care of their legal business before they took care of business. Now, you'd think that people would come to you more because of your name, but they won't. Instead, your customers would probably find themselves trying out the new Panda Express and loving it. Then, all of a sudden, you'd get a note in the mail or a call from Panda's lawyer saying "cease and desist using the name." How dare them? Well, they invested in the idea and they dove right in, but you just rented a building, bought a sign, and put out a few flyers. I see a lot of small and unregistered businesses on the Internet, and if I wanted to, I could give them a run for their money. I could take their name, create a larger company with it, and then invest in the idea. I could easily take over Google with their own name and cause their businesses to be found on page two or three of Google and my company's name on the first page. I wouldn't have to invest much money either. All I would have to do is start the business the right way, establish it, invest in it, and promote it. In addition, I could get a few customers, give them exceptional service, and then send them away to promote me through word of mouth. I'm not a thief, and I have my own ideas so they're safe, but there are many business owners and investors that aren't as nice as you or me. They will see a great concept put together with no time or money invested in it. They'll take that idea and run you out of your own country. Remember these words: investing is a round trip ticket, but spending is a one way ticket. Too many spenders are trying to start businesses. The error here is letting money direct you, when you should be directing your money.

Misconception #2: "No one can use my business name because I bought a domain name." A business name that is not registered can be used by anyone. To make matters worse, some names are common names and cannot be trademarked. A trademarked name has to be registered to the services that you are offering. For example, the company Tiffany's is registered as Tiffany & Co. Once you click the name, you'd find the list of services that they offer. Therefore, if I wanted to register a Tiffany's Company Computers; I could because I am specifying the type of business that I have, and it does not conflict with Tiffany & Company. If I wanted to open a Tiffany's Jewelry, that would be a conflict, and the U.S. Trademark would deny me. Nevertheless, if I came up with a company name that is not an actual word, I can easily trademark it for myself. I saw another guy use Apple Inc. as an example. He noted that Apple was able to register their name because the word "apple" has absolutely nothing to do with computers, but if someone actually had a company selling apples, the trademark would have been denied. Let's say, I decided to start a company called TifJewel. I'd get the trademark because TifJewel is not an actual word. If someone else tried to use TifJewel, they'd have a harder time registering the name because it is not a common name. So yes, someone can use your business's name, especially if it isn't trademarked. A trademark prevents them from using your company name and associating it with the same types of services that you offer. The error here is refusing to pay that $325 trademark fee. Sure, it's a steep price, but think of it this way: If your business went on to have earn $500,000 a year and someone else decided to tap into your pocketbook, they'd have no problem doing so. All they would have to do is register the business name and send you a cease and desist letter. And no, waiting to earn a certain amount isn't a wise idea, because there are people who scour the Internet looking for small businesses run by small-minded people, and they actually steal the business by registering it and investing in it. Someone may decide that they want to start a therapeutic pillow making business and want to find a good name for it, so they search the internet. Your business comes up and it's called, "Pillow Me Softly." Oh, what a catchy name it is! Then, your slogan reads, "P.M.S. reduces cramps." How sharp are you? So, they check U.S. Trademark and bingo! You haven't registered your business's name or slogan, so they'll do it for you. A few months later, you get a cease and desist note while they get your business. Don't be mad at them for having more faith in your idea than you did.

Misconception #3: "I can tell the people I love and trust about my idea, and they won't steal it." Three months later, you're wondering why your great idea is flashing on the television. People often find themselves acting as business coaches, only they are sharing their own business ideas and basically handing them to folks. Sometimes, the people you know won't steal your idea, but they too may have a big mouth. They'll tell someone they know about your great idea, and that someone tells someone they know, and before you know it, you need a new idea. Another error in telling people is that everyone isn't always happy for you. This includes your successful friends. Sometimes people learn to deal with you at a certain height, and they don't want to have to get to know you at a new height. You fit so well into their lives as you are. When you tell some folks, they'll speak against it, pray against it, and believe against it. Ladies, I know this is especially hard for you. The LORD gives you a business idea, and you want to tell your best friend, Erica. You're bubbling over with excitement, and you call her up to share the news. A few days later, for some reason, you feel drained, and the idea isn't as exciting anymore. When you told Erica, she sounded less than thrilled, so now you're thinking that it probably wasn't a good idea after all. I had to pray against my need to share what GOD had given to me. I purchased some twenty-cent notebooks and began to jot down what HE was giving me, and this was relieving to me. Nowadays, none of my friends know what I have in the works. They only find out when everyone else finds out; when the works are about to be published. It's not because they are bad people; it's because sometimes good people unintentionally do bad things, and no person will protect your baby like you will. The error here is singing like a bird while in the cage with a cat.

Misconception #4: "My sister, cousin, or best friend would make a great business partner or associate. I'm going to call him or her up and see if he or she wants in." More than 90 percent of businesses started with friends or family members fail. When GOD gives you an idea, you will feel driven and excited about the idea. That person you're trying to drag on board won't be so thrilled. Instead, all they will see is easy money, and all they will have is hope that you're right. I remember when I first started out in my business. I wanted so much to help the people that I loved so dearly. I started giving people I knew titles in my business and telling them all the great things I'd do for them once I "made it." I can't remember one of them even ever helping me out. They just had the title, but they didn't do any work. Then, I got this great idea to have a business partner. I wanted so badly to share the load so I wouldn't have to bear it by myself. This didn't work out either. I found myself working day in and day out to propel the business. I was excited about it and I knew it would do well, but that road had been carved out for me, and everyone else had their roads that they were supposed to be traveling.

The quickest way to make an enemy out of a friend is to try to put your hands in the same bank account. When people are familiar with you, they won't be as excited as someone who doesn't know you. They won't work as hard, and they definitely won't respect you or your ideas. Unless GOD tells you that your friend or family member is to come into business with you, don't let your emotions cause you to bring these people into business with you. If you do so, you'll come out with a testimony and, in most cases, it won't be a good one. That's a guarantee.

Misconception #5: "My business idea is going to make me rich!" The worst thing you can do is chase money. When you go into business looking to become rich, you'll be so focused on the peak of the mountain, that you won't pay attention to the climb. Eventually, you'll stumble and fall off that mountain. Everything that is designed starts off with a bottom step, and you have to walk your way to the top. You can't get to the top watching the top step; you have to pay attention to the steps ahead. Some businesses don't reach the million dollar mark for decades. The business may do okay for you, but it may serve as a gold mine for your children once you are gone from this earth. It is always a good idea to chase the knowledge and not the money. You may start a business teaching people how to swim and never see a million dollars from it, but if you wrote a book teaching people how to swim, you just may see a million dollars from that. Knowledge is far greater than any service or product you can offer. Wisdom is the principal thing. If you want to know how and where to find success; wisdom is it. There are many people that will have businesses just like yours, but if you have wisdom, knowledge, and understanding; you have set your business at the peak of the Master's heart, and no one can pull it down. *"Get wisdom, get understanding: forget it not; neither decline from the words of my mouth. Forsake her not, and she shall preserve thee: love her, and she shall keep thee. Wisdom is the principal thing; therefore get wisdom: and with all thy getting get understanding. Exalt her, and she shall promote thee: she shall bring thee to honour, when thou dost embrace her. She shall give to thine head an ornament of grace: a crown of glory shall she deliver to thee"* (Proverbs 4:5-9).

Misconception #6: "I should be earning enough money to quit my job within the next three months." Everything in this earth has to go through seasons. There is a season to sow and a season to reap. When you aren't bringing in much, it is obvious that you are in a season of sowing. This is when you need to sow a lot of time and money into what GOD has given you. You also need to sow time and money into helping others. For example, the widow and the orphans need you. Sowing is Kingdom principle. Don't sow because you want something in return, however. Sow because GOD told you to do so and because you love others as you love yourself. And you don't just have to sow money; sometimes, you can sow your time or sow wise counsel. Sowing is sacrifice; taking away from yourself to give to others.

Most people close their businesses because they didn't want to wait for the seasons to play out. They want fast money and fast success. I've mentored a few people who would quit in as little as one to three months when they didn't see any money coming in. Their reasoning was always, "I got bills to pay." Catch them in twenty years and they still got bills to pay. It is always easy to spot a winner; however, because they'll stay in it and believe in the vision that GOD has given them. They won't retreat no matter what circumstance plays out for them. Patience is absolutely fundamental to having a business.

Misconception #7: "My job wasn't paying me much, so I started my own business. I need consistent income because my bills are consistent." Before you quit your job, think about this truth: when owning your own business, you won't always net a consistent amount of money. Some months you'll do well and some months you may do poorly. Until you have set your foot on stable ground, it is better for you to keep your job and pay those consistent bills. Once your monthly income is more than enough to pay your bills and this income is consistent, *then* is a good time to consider turning in your two weeks notice. Don't run and quit your job just yet unless the LORD told you to do so. In this case, of course, you are to be obedient and just trust HIM.

Misconception #8: "I know I'm Christian, but GOD says not to judge, so I do business with the world as well. I created a pornographic site for the last guy, but it's not my site, so where is the sin?" Do you think Israel would have let the Egyptians built a city for them? You are either a Kingdom builder or you're on the other team. If you've got a doughnut and pastry shop, of course you can sell to the world. You are not promoting the world in doing so; you are simply feeding a hungry or greedy person. But when it comes to building, that's a different thing. If I was a construction worker, for example, I wouldn't mind building stores, gas stations, and houses; but if someone wanted to build a structure to promote sin, I wouldn't touch it with my forklift. Everyone's convictions aren't the same, but for me, I had to dedicate my hands to the LORD before HE blessed them. As a website builder, I wouldn't dare build a pornographic site, a gambling site, or even a site that promoted secular music. Read the following story for clarification: Donnie's dad, Joe, has a successful law firm. Donnie is going to law school to be a lawyer so that he can come into the practice with his dad. Across the street from the firm, another lawyer named Brad is establishing his practice, and he's got his sights on Joe's law firm. He knows that Joe gets some pretty well-known and high-end clients, so he positions his business where he can see who comes in and out and see if he could steal them. One day, Brad spots Donnie outside and asks him if he'd like to come to work for him. He'd pay him more than his dad was giving him, and he'd even start him off with a huge bonus. Donnie agrees, and he takes the knowledge that he acquired from his dad and helps to propel Brad's law firm to the top. How do you feel about Donnie at this very moment? How dare he go to work for his father's enemy and take the knowledge that his father had given him to his enemy. Now Joe's law firm is in danger because his son is working for the enemy. Sometimes, we have to see it from a worldly point of view that we can relate to before we can understand the sting of it. You can't serve GOD and mammon (money). You will come to that fork in the road that has claimed many Christian souls. There will be two roads to choose from. On one road, you'll see dollar signs doing their seductive dance and wolves waving steaks at a hungry you. On the other road, there will be nothing in view, but faith will whisper in the winds, "Just follow the road." Truthfully, more than 75 percent of people take the wrong road because they wanted to get to the testimony before they finished enduring the tests. They go down these roads and get a taste of a few hundred or a few thousand bucks before lack shuts them in and cuts off the lights. This book is to teach you how to run a *successful* Christian business, not just how to run a Christian business. The two aren't the same. Anything you do for GOD has to glorify HIM and HIM only. This decision isn't an easy one (for most) when lack is telling you that it needs to be fed, but your love for GOD and your faith in HIM will always cause you to make the right decision. If you find yourself negotiating with your need and making excuses, you're on the wrong road. Not trusting GOD is always a fatal error.

<u>Your Worst Customer</u>

The greatest sale you will ever make with your business is to sell yourself. Not just to others, but to yourself. As human beings, we tend to be afraid of the unknown; therefore, we visit the edges of unfamiliarity, but many never go into the depths of the unknown to embrace a new day. Again, it is fear that causes us to focus on what we know and to stay away from what we don't know. Once you have convinced yourself that you'd make a great business owner and that you can succeed, the hardest thing is staying confident when you visit the lows of business ownership. These are the times when you don't see a profit or don't see a reasonable profit. These low times are also the times when you find yourself negotiating down your price and chasing up behind potential customers.

One thing that you need to immediately understand about those low times is that you are often the cause of them. Sure, there's an offending bite to that remark, considering you may be doing all that you <u>know how</u> to do to succeed, but keep finding yourself in the grips of failure. This simply means you need more information to continue. In addition, it isn't what you know that causes you to succeed, it the consistent application of that knowledge coupled with an unyielding faith that brings about growth. Likewise, it isn't always what you don't know that causes you to fail; it is what you don't want to know and what you refuse to apply. For example, people often find it hard to set rules in place and stick to them, so they don't know how much money they are losing out on because of their lack of order. They focus more on what money they are trying to get from one person as opposed to what they could earn from a multitude of customers. I'll demonstrate through example:

Jeremy really needs to get up the funds to pay his car note. He is a business owner, and he's a little desperate today. Mark is negotiating with Jeremy about Jeremy's consulting prices. He wants to pay $300 total for a few sessions, whereas Jeremy charges $499. Jeremy's car payment is past due, so Jeremy is considering taking Mark up on his offer. This negotiation has been in the makings for more than a week now, and Mark is wearing Jeremy down. If Jeremy negotiates, he'd have the money for his car payment, but nothing else. So, Jeremy takes the offer and Mark becomes his client.

Mark is a difficult client. He wants all that he can get, plus more. Unlike Jeremy's customers that happily paid the $499, Mark is tedious, demanding, and confrontational. Jeremy immediately regrets charging down the offer, but has to deal with Mark until the contract is complete.

Now, I know that most people would say that they would have done like Jeremy and took the offer because their car note was due. You're going to get a lot of Marks in your day-to-day operations, but let's revisit the facts: Jeremy has been allowing this negotiation to take place for over a week. This is valuable time that he could have been advertising his business, but he gave Mark way too much of his time. Mark didn't want to honor Jeremy's rules or pricing; therefore, Jeremy should have firmly stated his pricing and stayed there. Had he done it, Mark would have probably went ahead and hired him, and if he didn't, good riddance. People like Mark close down many small businesses every day because of how they view those businesses. When some people see your business as a home-grown business, they won't respect it. They feel that you have no right to have rules, prices set in concrete, and so on. Therefore, they try to deal with you on a personal level rather than a professional level. This is where you step in to either correct or confirm their beliefs. Sure, you'll lose some customers, but some money simply costs too much! And many times, these types of customers actually cost you more money than they are paying you. Do the math and you'll see. This is why so many Christian businesses end up closing. It's not because of customers like Mark, but it is more so because of owners like Jeremy. There are many people who will try to get over on you. Don't be surprised that they are Christian, and don't be surprised that many are Christians with leadership titles. Every human being alive has some fault to him or her, and oftentimes you will find what their hangup is when you are dealing with their money.

The responsibility of keeping your doors open falls upon you. You can let fear, lack, and greed offer you a quick settlement while they systematically close down your business; or you can let faith advise you to stick to your rules and look for the long term results. Businesses that operate like garage sales usually don't stay open long, and the owner often blames the customers. It's not the customer's fault. If a man could go into an ice cream shop and talk them into letting him pay a dime for an ice cream sundae, then he will. That shop would be filled to the brim with happy cheap customers and would, of course, go out of business. But, go into any established ice cream parlor, and you'll find that you have to pay what they require of you to get that ice cream cone. It's the same with a gas station. Sure, you can fill up your car, but you'd better go in and pay or you'll end up in jail. Larger companies set their rates and they do not back down from them. Why do they not negotiate with the "hard on their luck" souls that wander into them? Because, in business and in life, every transaction is a trade-off. People trade their dollars for your products and services. The person offering the products or services is supposed to walk away with enough money to purchase whatever they need and still make a profit. That's the trade-off. If someone walks up to you and they are in "a situation" and you sow into their "situation," you're going to end up with a similar "situation." Sure, go out and give to the poor, but giving and doing business are two different things. If you don't believe this, then head into a gas station and tell them about your "situation." Show them your teary eyes and the pictures of your hungry kids and then go pump some gas. Go back into the gas station and say, "Thank you so much for helping me out. My car is now full and I'll be able to take my kids to school and go looking for a job this week. That was free, right?" Watch the looks you'll get. If you leave, your situation won't improve because you'll have a whole new situation to consider: finding bail money and a decent attorney. Hopefully, he'll understand your "situation" and give you a break on his fee.

Do not establish short-term business relationships that are scheduled to become ugly break-ups. Think about a romantic relationship. Would you go out and purposely date a man or a woman that you knew was a two-timer? If you met a person and was considering a relationship with them, but you saw them out one day with a romantic interest that you knew nothing of, you'd probably dump them and keep on living. You know that this person will become a two-timing permanent marker in your life that is just going to keep on hurting you if you allow them to continue in your life. If a cheating partner isn't what you want, you'd flee. Business works the same way. You will come across potential or actual customers who will come to the storefront as a problem. To continue on with them is error, because not only will they take up too much of your time, but they will eventually walk away and bad mouth you. You may spend years gracefully and politely dealing with their abrasive speech and their sarcasms and then, all of a sudden, one day you will make a minor error. Let's say, for example, you did their dry cleaning, and one day you accidentally overcharged them twenty-five cents. You put the wrong code into the cash register because you were overwhelmed and trying to hurry them on out of the store. They immediately notice the error and accuse you of trying to rob them, so they vow never to do business with you again, and they then go on to blog about how terrible of a business that you are running. If you were to read their blog, you'd find that their blog is full of rants about local businesses that didn't do what they demanded. You're in a predicament; however, because you tolerated this person for a few years, and now they have the inside scoop about your business. Every time they came to your storefront, they were rude and took up a lot more time than your normal customers, but you gave it to them in hopes of keeping their business. Not to mention, this character never likes to pay you full price for the work that you've done. He finds a hair snag in his pants that was probably there before and demands a refund, so you give it to him. Another time, he finds a stain in his shirt that simply could not be removed and he continues to ridicule you until you refund him. And then, there are those times when he walks away without a complaint and these days are relieving to you. Every time he comes into your store, you feel a dark cloud come over you. You just want to finish his order and send him away without incident, but it's a toss-up with this guy; one day he's a jerk, and another day he smiles at you and bad-mouths the business next door. This is not a customer that you want to keep, because eventually he'll do more harm than good. You don't want that day to come when you just can't bite your tongue any longer, and you empower him by contending with him. Instead, it would have been better if his blog post stated that you refused to do business with him than that you'd done business with him, but your services were horrible. Pay attention to the larger stores and how they handle such customers. They may initially do business with such a character, and even try to overlook that customer's attitude, but eventually, once his antics become common knowledge, he's run off by their refusal to submit to his demands.

When I first started doing business, I came across some of the worst of the worst. As a woman, I found that some of the women I worked with would be very condescending and speak in such a rude and prideful tone towards me. I had a couple of women who tried to send me a logo that someone else had done, trying to school me about how a logo is "supposed to look." Of course, I politely refunded their money and told them to hire the designer of those logos because I'm only anointed to be Tiffany. Many men that I came in contact with were flirtatious and tried to con work out of me. Yes, these were self-professed Christians! I had people that basically told me how they wanted to do business with me and I accepted it, trying to get the money. As GOD elevated me, HE taught me to trust in HIM only. These people weren't my providers; they were hindrances that didn't need to be a part of my Rolodex.

How do you deal with such a customer? What do you do when your bills are due and this customer is waving what you need in front of your nose, but all you have to do is meet their ridiculous demands? Here are a few tips that you'll have to take by faith:
1. Remember that all money isn't what it portrays itself to be. Some money costs too much to get. If their attitude or demands aren't worth the hassle, send them away. A nice way to decline working with someone is to send them to someone else in that field. If you're busy, say you're busy and send them away. Sure, they'll be frustrated with you, but your sanity is priceless.
2. Use idle time to advertise. Rather than trying to grab a hold of money that you can see, sometimes it is better to open the hands of your faith to receive the money that you can't see. If business isn't booming, place an ad in the paper. Do something that you've never done before, or do something that you have done before and saw results.
3. Sometimes a rude customer can become a law-abiding customer when you place rules down and refuse to go outside of them. This is a very important rule. Think about how tough the criminal justice system is in Texas. Some career criminals actually move to Texas and try to straighten up because the penalties are a lot tougher for the crimes that they've made a career of committing. Some children are horrible towards their

parents because there is no discipline or no consistent discipline in the home, but those same children are like angels with other family members. Whereas Mommy might be patiently hoping that Bryon will grow out of his rebellious ways and unbridled tongue, Aunt Helen may not be as patient. Aunt Helen believes in consistent discipline and tough love, so Bryon gives her all of his love and tries endlessly to please her. Your customers will oftentimes be the same way. In other words, people will do what you allow them to do, but when you put rules in place and refuse to break them; your customer will either abide by them or walk away and become someone else's problem.

4. Faith is funny like that. Sometimes, you can't see what you need, so you have to believe GOD for it. GOD will allow you to accept the "headache money" from the small business assassin that has placed his money on closing your business, but it is better to glorify HIS Name by believing HIM for provision. Some people would contend with this, believing that the rude customer is a GOD-send in disguise, but just do the research. Find about five small businesses that ended up closing their doors and ask them what they believe caused the destruction of their businesses. Many times, it was simply negotiating with the devil himself.

5. Never chase money. As a Christian, you are to always seek ye first the Kingdom of GOD and all its righteousness and trust that everything else will be added onto you as declared in Matthew 6:33. Money always follows a believer that follows GOD. Money is designed to run and hide from the unbeliever and the Christian that has trouble believing GOD. But money pursues the righteous to the point where they can't get away from it. They are cornered on every side by the blessings of GOD. They are overtaken by the love of GOD and overshadowed by the favor of GOD.

There are also customers that are extremely manipulative. They can be super friendly and super manipulative all in the same breath. A woman may come along and pretend to be your friend; it happens all the time. But in reality, she's a non-paying client in disguise. She's come to spy out your business and sift your brain for ideas. She has also come for free services. These are the demands of her friendship.

As my business grew, I had many men and women alike that tried to attach to me. In the beginning, being naïve, I would welcome the chats and then the phone calls. Then, I would hear the pity stories that are their lives. I wanted to help, but I knew that I could not help them out financially or by doing the work for them freely, so I would try to push them into their own gifted corners. This did not work out the way it played out in my head because many people don't want to do the work associated with business ownership; they simply want the rewards. I tried to push them and I tried to encourage them, but it was like trying to crank up a car with a bad battery; there would be a spark, and then nothing. Eventually, these people would stop calling me, and I even had one or two to delete me (Facebook) because I refused to do a free service for them. After all, I knew their situation. Many of them weren't working, and it was an insult to them for me to ask for payment. These people were manipulative, and their foundation was not trusting GOD for provision; it was trusting in their own devices and trusting in other people. This is what you will commonly deal with, and you have to absolutely prepare yourself for it. These are customers that do not want to pay for services. This is why they have "situations."

Another manipulative customer is the one that does not want to pay the posted pricing or does not want to abide by the rules. So, they'll pretend not to see the prices or the rules, and they'll try to go around them. Never ever let this work in your business, as it will cause your business to become like a garage sale or an under-the-table operation. One of the things that the LORD told me was to never let someone deal with me like they deal with a man selling boot-legged CDs. Instead, what you are to do is keep your business clean. You wouldn't allow dirt to gather on your floor. You'd clean it up and try to keep it clean so that you can be comfortable and your customers can be comfortable. Do the same with your business dealings. Try to keep and maintain your paying, non-problematic customers, and let your rules sweep away the other ones. And remember: there is one who comes in through the door because he was invited, but anyone that tries to come through the window is a thief.

One more form of manipulation worth mentioning is when a customer threatens to ruin you or your business if you don't do as you're told by them. When you start to do business in a major way, you will get this character more than likely. What if you have 225 positive reviews on Google, and you've been loving your perfect score, but now, here is this customer threatening to be your first negative review, and they intend to post up negative comments on other sites? Let them! Stay within the protective barriers of your rules and understand that negative attention does not always yield negative results. There are many people who read negative reviews, and these people would not have ordinarily come to your business, but the review caught their attention, and they wanted to see who you were. In walking into the building or logging onto your website, they have found that you have 225 positive reviews, plus your services are great! One negative review will ultimately bring you at least 10 customers! Yes, there are a few that will refuse to do business with you because of that review, but chances are, they weren't going to do business with you anyway. Any person that sees 225 positive reviews but focuses on that one negative review is a negative person. Why focus on them? Your goal should always be to gather and retain positive, paying customers who know what they want and appreciate what you give. This is one of the most common complaints that I get from business owners. They get a rude or manipulative customer, and they try to hold on to them. They go to the ends of their patience trying to bleed that little money out of them, and they find that even after the services have been rendered, the customer continues to harass them. This is very common with clients of web designers, for example. A client will pay for and get a website. End of story, right? No, oftentimes, it is the beginning of the designer's nightmare if they don't have rules in place. The client calls back, trying to get more work on the site, but doesn't want to understand that they have to pay for updates and redesigns. After relaying this to the customer over and over again, most web designers begin to ignore that customer's phone calls. After all, they don't want to pay for the update; they simply want the designer to do the work as a favor, and they'll talk for hours trying to convince the designer to do the work. That designer, instead, focuses on his or her paying clients and lets the freebie stalker go to voicemail to leave yet another desperate message. After a few weeks or months, the client finally catches on and leaves a voicemail stating that they are ready to pay for the update. It is then that they get a call back if the designer hasn't by then blocked them. Many times, the client will go and hire a new designer to create a new site for them or ask the old designer to transfer the login information to their new designer. Find them in a few years, and they've been through quite a few designers because they believe that they shouldn't have to pay for updates...ever. They've aided in closing down many Christian businesses, and they could not care less about you having mouths to feed.

The message here is understand that even when you earn, you are paying something. If what you are paying is more than what you are to earn, don't take the job. If you do, make sure that the customer understands that you have rules, and that you do not go outside of these rules. You don't have to verbalize this; you can state this in a contract and require that the customer sign and return the contract stating that they've read, understand, and will comply with what is written in the contract. This won't necessarily free you from their vengeful wrath, but it will legally protect you from them. Most of them won't read the contract or read the rules on the website, but my motto is: not reading the rules does not make you exempt from them. When a customer tells me that they didn't know that this rule was in place and insists on me overriding it because they chose not to read the contract or the website, I refer them back to my rules. Of course, they are less likely to do any more business with me after that, but this isn't necessarily a bad thing. One bad customer will always distract you from hundreds of potential good customers, but fear will make you focus on a few hundred dollars, whereas faith will help you to see the big picture.

<u>Your Worst Enemy</u>

In business, you are your own worst enemy because everything in life is choice-driven. When you make the wrong choices, you get the wrong results. Business owners tend to think too hard or not hard enough, but it takes GOD to teach you to find your stable footing in the business world.

Have you ever been shopping in a store and a few items just turned you off completely? You may have had a few items in your hand or in your shopping cart, but after running into a few tasteless items, you suddenly lost your shopping drive and decided to go elsewhere. Have you ever called a restaurant to place an order and changed your mind because the person that answered the phone wasn't so nice? Have you ever went to a website to shop it but were turned off by its look, so you closed the site? This is common with businesses. All of the customers that come to do business with you aren't stable in their decision to do business with you. For example, a woman may head out to shop for shoes to wear to a wedding. She may enter your shop and find that there's an odd smell in the store, your store looks more like a thrift shop than a retail outlet, and you've got the family dog sitting by the counter looking unpredictable. Consequently, she just may leave in search of a better looking, better smelling store that understands that people like her are allergic to animal dander. As a shop owner, you may be firmly set on doing business your way, but being inconsiderate towards your potential customers is entrepreneurial suicide.

Look at some of the largest companies that specialize in what you specialize in, and ask yourself what makes them different from you, besides their success. What makes them successful? What do they have that you don't have? The average person would name the things that this business has, but in reality, the leadership has a plan; a different way of thinking and marketing than you do. If you took that same team of people and gave them only what you have, they'd more than likely turn it into success because they know how to. Your goal is to learn more than what they know. Knowing what the average company knows only floats you alongside those companies, but knowing and providing more serves as an anchor to your company and allows you to charge higher or lower rates at your discretion.

The problem with most Christian business owners that I've come in contact with is money management. Most Christian entrepreneurs refuse to invest a decent amount of money into their companies. When asked why, many of them say that they are in business to make money, not to lose it. This mindset serves as a weapon in their hand against their own companies, because when you refuse to invest in your company, it shows. As a result, you will come across a lot of low-budget looking Christian companies and websites that are proudly promoted by people wearing the best attire. They will happily cover themselves in riches and place this huge photo of themselves dressed to impress on the front page of their websites, but their websites look like they were built as a joke. You have to realize that you are not for sale, but what you are offering is for sale. This is where a lot of first-time business owners get confused because, quite naturally, you're going to be excited at the prospect of having your own business. A lot of times, people forget to market their businesses, services, and products as much as they market themselves. In tutoring new business owners, I often have had to get to the root of why some of the new owners were insistent about filling their website up with pictures of themselves. One thing that you have to realize is that your customers won't be interested in pictures of you unless they relate to what you are offering. The only people that will come to your website to look at your pictures will be people that know you personally. You can create a Facebook page for that and save yourself the extra money of adding those pages to the site. You should never combine your business thinking with your personal thinking. Serious business owners don't place photos of themselves on their business sites, but they will place them on their personal sites. For example, when I first launched out, I used my name dot com as my personal and business site because I didn't know any better. As GOD grew me up, I began to separate my business site from my personal site. I displayed all of my services on my personal site, but they were all linked to my other sites. That's because when we learn better, we do better.

Presentation is very important in a business. How you present your business and yourself will determine how others view you. If you present yourself the wrong way, you will harm your business.

People often launch out with low-budget looking setups because they plan to upgrade later, but presentation starts the first day that you go into business. It is then that you are starting to build your crowd, your name, and your reputation. If you start out looking and presenting yourself one way, the crowd that frequents you will not be too pleased when you decide to upgrade your business, because this means higher pricing and more rules. This is when you just may lose your customers; therefore, to avoid having this transitional time where you have to go and look for new customers, you should just start out right the first time. The problem is never a lack of funds; the problem is always a lack of knowledge. Someone with limited funds that has read, researched, and compared their market will find better deals, but someone that is just trying to find something to fit their budget will take whatever is thrown at them.

<u>Sequential or Consequential Order</u>

In worldly establishments, you will find that there is a first-come, first-serve rule that is honored, but isn't always followed. For example, if you go to KFC and order honey barbeque wings and there aren't any ready, they'll take your payment and have you get out of the line. They'll more than likely tell you the wait time, and while you wait, they will serve other customers. Why don't they just wait until your food is ready before serving other customers? Because they want to keep those customers. You are one person, and they desire to keep you as a customer, but any good business would rather lose one customer than 30. If they could have served 30 customers in the time it took to prepare your meal, but they chose to follow the first-come-first-serve rule, they'd more than likely lose 30 customers.

I have found that in Christian establishments, some people try to honor this first-come-first-serve rule to remain fair to their customers, and as a consequence, they end up losing the customers that they made wait. Think of this scenario: You have a Christian company that sells perfume, and Phil wants to buy 30 boxes of your perfume. You don't have 30 boxes in stock, so you give Phil a time in which the products should be available. You do have 10 boxes in stock, however. In addition, you have two customers that want three bottles each, but you chose to give the 10 boxes to Phil, so now your other customers have to wait as well. If the perfume that you are selling is in stock with another buyer, you will more than likely lose your customers to that buyer. The right way to do business is to go ahead and fill the orders that you can fill quickly and apologize to Phil for making him wait. Some would say that they would give Phil those 10 boxes of perfume and have him wait for the rest, but for what? His order still has not been completely filled; therefore, he may still go elsewhere along with the two customers that you chose to put off with him. In this situation, you should have acted like KFC and served the customers that you could serve for now and offered Phil a free bottle of perfume with his order or a discount. Sometimes, you wouldn't even have to offer him anything because Phil may have already known that you wouldn't have 30 bottles in stock, so he was willing to wait.

As a business owner, I oftentimes contract with other business owners to take on some of the extra services that I have. Especially if I have a load of customers. I love to work with climbing businesses because I love to see Christian businesses excel, but many times, I find out why these businesses stay on the rocks and keep falling off. They keep trying to honor sequential order, and consequentially; they lose their customers. I have found that many small businesses are run by people with small minds. Now, this is not to insult you if you've made a few mistakes in your business. We all make mistakes and this is how we learn, but some people don't learn from their mistakes, they continually repeat them until repetition runs them out of business. It doesn't matter if you are offering a tangible product or a service, always serve the customers whom you can serve quickly at first, and then take care of the customers who require more time. That way, you don't have what I refer to as order pile-up. Anytime I contract with a business to perform a service for me, and they take longer than one of their competitors would have because of other orders, I don't work with them anymore.

For example, I have a seal and logo store that currently has more than 600 designs in it. I pre-designed these graphics so that my customers could shop freely without worrying about if they'd like the design or not. Many of my customers shop the store, and then there are the ones who request a custom design. Now, the ones in my store are ready to buy; all I have to do is add the text to them, but a custom design, I have to put together based on the customer's request. I frequently get customers that order custom designs and customers that come along after them and want a design from my store. What am I to do? I immediately put the text on the pre-designed graphics and send them out to my customers, and then I begin the custom design. Why? Because the latter order would not affect the first order, but the first order could affect the latter one. This order has helped me to keep all of my customers happy, since they all receive their designs in the times agreed upon or, in most cases, earlier. If I have a web design client that wants a three page website and another one that wants a seven page website, I would follow the sequential order because I can still fill each order in the time frame that I gave to each customer. Now, the first customer may be a difficult one. For example, she wants me to go and save her images from online, create a Facebook fan page for her, create a Twitter account, and so on. In this case, I'll go ahead and take care of my latter customer because they aren't requiring as much time or work. The goal here is to provide services for both customers in a timely manner instead of lining them up like school children out for play.

You shouldn't bring your customers to the front of the line because of favor, however, but you should always look at the workload and calculate how much time and effort each customer is going to require. Always strive to perform the services or provide the products in a timely manner. If you give your customers the services and products that they've ordered on time, you're late in the eyes of the customer because your competitors would have happily given them a better product in a more timely fashion, in many cases, for less than what you're offering.

Remember, trying to be sequential can have consequential results. Always think about your customers' happiness first, rather than trying to line them up. Sometimes, when you allow order pile-up to overcome you, you won't do your best work because you'll try to speed things up to deliver to each customer in a timely fashion. This is worker's anxiety, and it makes you eager to complete the work or be sluggish, because depression can and does start to set in on many business owners when they get order pile-up. Getting a lot of orders is a good thing, but if you don't know how to manage them, you're in trouble.

<u>The Wrong Price</u>

Over the years, I have experimented with pricing. I have often offered up promotions and discounts to test the market and see just what my target audience needs. Sure, I could research the Internet and pull up the statistical findings of someone else, but I prefer to test the market myself so that I can see what works and does not work for my company. Sometimes, general statistics just aren't for you, because there are many denominators that may exclude you from the findings. For example, if the study was conducted on middle-classed Caucasians and you happen to be African American with an audience comprised primarily of African Americans, the findings won't reflect the ideas and behaviors of your target audience. So, to apply those findings to your business could mean professional suicide.

Anyhow, I was surprised at what I found when conducting my studies. I learned that every time I took my prices down, I would lose sales, but any time I took my prices up, my sales would increase. I was absolutely floored by this because there were times when I thought maybe I needed to go down on my prices. Another interesting fact that I discovered was the class of customers I would get when I took my prices down. Anytime I lowered the prices of my logos, I would get some of the most conniving and manipulative customers. Again, my sales would go down, and many of the customers that I did get would be a nightmare to work with. In such cases, most of the customers did not want to abide by the rules, and more than 50% of them tried to find a way to get the logos for even less. And because I require a 50% deposit up front, I would get bombarded by protests from the customer about paying the required deposit. The deposit alone would shave away 80% of my potential customers. Many of the ones that did stick around, however, would scream bloody murder or go into hiding when the balance was requested. Of course, because they'd paid a non-refundable deposit, they'd always end up paying the balance rather than losing the logo and their money. So, when they came out of hiding, they would often have an excuse as to why they've been missing for a few weeks. The most common excuse I got was either someone they know passed away, or that they'd got sick. After a while, these stories became so commonplace that I already knew what the customer was going to say before they said it. Did someone actually die? Probably so; people die every day, but oftentimes, these aren't people they have a relationship or a close relationship with. Did the customer get sick? Probably so, but it wasn't an illness that kept them from going to work. The problem was that they had a wrongful relationship with money, and this is why they would only order logos that were placed within their limited reach.

How much should you charge for your business? That's a question that many have, but the answer is different for everyone because your prices would depend on:
- The services or products you offer.
- Your target audience.
- Your available audience.
- The prices set forth by companies who provide similar products and services.
- Your skill level.

The Services and Products You Offer

Of course, you would have to research the services and products you offer. Oftentimes, people go into business looking at their competitor's prices, and they base their prices around their competitor's prices. This is absolute error because your competitor may have a different skill level and a different audience than you do. You need to look at the costs to you and the time you'll spend performing the duties that are expected of you. When you end up under-charging, you'll lose interest in the business itself because you'll find yourself working hard and earning little. A great way to come up with a price draft is to look at EVERY fee that you are going to have to put forth running your business. How much does it cost you to continually run that business? How much are you paying for products, licenses, taxes, and other fees weekly or monthly? How much gas are you using in your vehicle? How much time are you spending doing the work? One of the biggest mistakes first time business owners make is when they project their costs based on ONLY what they spent and forget to pay themselves. How much do you want to make each day, each week, and every month? This has to be taken into consideration. If you paid $10,000 to launch the company, how long do you project that you will have earned at least that amount back? It is only after you earn your initial investment back that you can start seeing a profit, and oftentimes, this takes up to two or more years. What are you going to do to earn your initial investment back, and how are you going to front the costs of running that business until the business begins to pay for itself?

Your Target Audience

Who are you targeting? If you don't know your target audience, you will undoubtedly go out of business and fast. You wouldn't go to a nursing home trying to sell car insurance to the patients, would you? Of course not. Most, if not all, of the people there aren't driving anymore.

Knowing your target audience is extremely important when

setting up your prices. If you go into a neighborhood, set up a restaurant, and start selling cheeseburger combos, you need to know what the people in your area can afford since your restaurant is targeting them. You would have to research other restaurants in your area to see what people are accustomed to paying. Then, you would have to research and determine which restaurants get the most business and why. Let's say the area you are set up in has a Joe's Burger Joint and a Sally's Burger Hut. Joe's cheeseburger combos are $4.99, and they come with a double stacked cheeseburger, fries, and a medium drink. Sally's cheeseburger combos are $6.99 and they come with a double stacked cheeseburger, fries, and a large drink. In your research, you find that Sally's Burger Hut gets more business. Now, you need to find out why they get more business than Joe's. Sally's combos are $2 more than Joe's, and one would think that if it was the large drink that sent people flooding into Sally's, they'd realize they are paying for that large drink. Your research is over, and after surveying more than 100 people in your area, you find that Sally's hamburgers taste better than Joe's. Plus Joe's staff is pretty rude, and people don't like dealing with their attitudes. What is it about Sally's cheeseburgers that makes them better? It could be a secret sauce, or maybe Sally uses a different kind of beef. After your research, you can put your burger joint together offering your own secret sauce, friendlier staff, and you'll know the general attitude of your target audience. This would undoubtedly give you an edge over the burger joints in your area because you didn't just set up a burger joint; you took the time out to see what your future customers wanted. In addition, you took the time out to connect with your future customers and establish a bond with them that they won't soon forget. People like to know that they are being heard, appreciated, and considered.

Your Available Audience

This is where many people get confused, because most business coaches will only tell you how to find your target audience, but no one is talking about the most important audience: your available audience.

Let's say that you opened up a booth in your local mall. There are two malls in your city. One of them is where the upper middle-class and the wealthy frequent, and the other is the mall where the lower middle-class and the poor frequent. For example, we'll call the mall for the upper middle class and the wealthy "The Palace," and we'll call the mall for the lower middle class and the poor "Royal Quarters." You happen to set up your booth in Royal Quarters to sell your new makeup line. You have created this highly-pigmented eye shadow that triumphs over MAC®, and your dream is to sell it for double the price of MAC® eye shadows. So, your single eye shadows starts at $50. That's expensive, but you know your product is worth it. Anyhow, if you sold that eye shadow for $50 in the Royal Quarters, you'll probably make one sale a week. If that's not bad enough, then what would be even worse is when that one customer attempts to get a refund because they got home and realized that they couldn't afford to pay $50 for eye shadow. You couldn't get mad at the people for not buying your eye shadows. You went into a common mall with high-end products trying to sell them for prices that many of your customers cannot afford. These customers are your available audience.

So, what should one do in a situation where they have high-end products but can only afford to market them in places where they won't get their asking price? It's simple; either you change your price, or you change your location. A wise thing to do is to change your price and introduce your product to the consumers that are available to you. If your product is good, the people will keep coming back for them. You could save up your earnings to prepare the product for your target audience. After your product has made a name for itself, and you can afford to suffer the initial hit of starting afresh amongst a whole new audience, then you could move and begin to establish your name amongst your target audience.

Always remember to discern between your target audience and your available audience. If you can afford to, and you are patient enough to market only to your target audience; do so. But, if you need money now and you want to start making sales immediately, you will have to market your products to your available audience.

The Prices Set Forth By Companies Who Provide Similar Products and Services

One of the things that I always teach entrepreneurs is to never see other Christian businesses as their competitors because it will only distract them from being as blessed as they individually are. Nevertheless, as an entrepreneur, you should know the price of what others would refer to as your competitors. The reason for this is that most people have a comfort zone in relation to how much they spend for a particular service or product. This comfort zone was established by the companies that they generally do business with. If you come on the scene charging prices that go outside of what they are comfortable paying, most people won't even give your business a chance to prove itself worthy of the hire.

First, you will need to research the price of companies in your area if you have a local business. People in your area will often frequent those businesses; therefore, they have a certain price range that you need to abide by for now. You could charge a little more or a little less, but make sure what you are offering is worth what you are asking.

Next, you need to research the general price of the services and products you offer; extending your research to companies within a certain mile radius, and then a national average. This will let you know what you can eventually charge, and where you need to market your products or services to charge the national average. Additionally, you should research other products and services that you can give as bonuses or add-ons.

Your Skill Level

A lot of people forget this very important rule of running a business. Your prices should always be determined by your skill level. As you level up, your prices should go up. When you are a rookie, you shouldn't charge professional prices. One of the worst (and funniest) flops I see many Christian business owners make is attempting to sell low-grade products and services for higher prices than that of which a professional charges. It's funny because I can relate to their initial mentality. People often see business ownership as a way to get rich quick, and they calculate how much money they spent and how much money they want to make. The worst math you can do is to calculate how many customers you'll need to earn a certain amount after overcharging them. It's okay to calculate how many customers you'll need to earn a certain amount, but when you have to take up your prices to reach a certain goal, you'll run your customers off.

You can't charge the same amount as your neighboring business if their skill level is higher than yours. Books are a great example. I've seen people come out with their first book and get big-headed before their first sale. I've seen ebooks on sale for $25. These were 30 page ebooks by a new and unknown author. Of course, the authors weren't educated about the market before casting their lines out, so they planned their retirement and waited for a miracle. 100 books at $25 is $2,500! The funniest part is that every one of these authors refused to invest in the production and editing of their books. That's why they put out ebooks only. They were considered rookie authors because they were new, and yet they charged more than T.D. Jakes for the very same information. When marketing yourself, your products, or your services, you should always consider your skill level. When you are new to the business, you first have to establish your company's name as a new player in the arena. Then, you have to establish your company's name as either another player or a major player in that business arena. You do this by learning more and more about the products and services you are offering, and by adding new products and services to your list often.

There are many things you need to consider before setting your product or service's price, but always remember that charging too much will run you out of business. Charging too little will only invite in people who have a wrongful relationship with money, and they will run you out of business because they want what you have to offer, but they don't want to let go of their money. Even after they've given that money to you in exchange for a product or a service, they will still refer to it as "my money" because people who have a wrongful relationship with money have trouble releasing it from their hands and their hearts.

If you are going to establish a business amongst people who have wrongful relationships with money, you'd better learn some warfare prayers and learn how to deal with aggressive customers. My advice is to always market in the middle or at the top. Of course, this will cost you more money to setup and run, but eventually, it'll bring you more profit as well. Additionally, you won't have to deal too much with customers who love their money more than they love your life or lifestyle.

Research the business and don't be anxious to launch yourself out there. Proper studies will give you the information that you need to not just start your business, but become an established business owner who doesn't flinch at the sight of opposition.

Other things to take into consideration when setting your prices are:
- **Customer demand:** Determine whether your product or service is needed, and how important it is to consumers.
- **Supply and demand:** Are the products you sell easy to obtain? What about consumer demand for those products or services?
- **Possible fluctuation in supply pricing:** Some of your supplies may be coming from external companies.

Watch the market and prepare yourself accordingly. Oftentimes, as the price of fuel goes up, so will the price of tangible products. Look for other companies that you may use in case one company goes up on their prices. Their choice to do so could run you out of business if they are your only supplier.

- **Evolution of the marketplace:** As computers and digital products continue to get smarter, new products will surface that will quickly become the best-sellers of the marketplace. Always stay up-to-date, or better yet, stay ahead of the times and adjust your prices to fit the ever evolving market.

<u>**Rebellion**</u>

Throughout this book, you will see me elaborate on having rules and staying within the safe confines of those rules. At first, I didn't know how vital having and applying rules was to the survival of my business. That's because every new thing we start, we start as a rookie. First, it took me a while to believe GOD and set some rules. Then, after getting financially and spiritually dragged through the mud, I finally surrendered and set some rules. Next, I rebelled against my own rules. I would bend one and break two rules just to appease a trying customer. I figured that since they were giving me what I wanted, I had to give them what they wanted. Because of this way of thinking, I had plenty of customers who took advantage of me, and each time I would try to justify giving in. After all, they did pay me for a service. Even though I'd performed that service over and over again, I still felt obligated to them. Nevertheless, after finally completing each of these orders, I would feel drained. I was on the ropes, and I had been worn out. Something was contending with me, but I didn't realize that initially. I had to go through it again and again until I got tired.

What was contending with me? The spirit of rebellion. Please know that rebellion is real, and it attacks Christian ministries and businesses in the same way that leeches attack fish. It attaches to its host and begins to drain them in every way. When I realized that I had been submitting to the rebellion in people, I immediately stopped, and I started to stand by my rules.

Please understand that your rules are on your side. They are there to protect you. You don't go against your rules; you stand with them. There are many people who are bound by rebellion, and they absolutely love to take advantage of Christian businesses. Anytime they deal with a Christian business; they refuse to follow the rules. They have to add their input, and they have to get you to do over whatever it is that they wanted you to do. It's never right the first time with them. The truth is: They want power and control over GOD'S anointed. This charges them up and they are addicted to power. If you feed into their spirit, they will never release you because you have become a source of power for them, and you are now feeding their addiction.

Case and point: I occasionally will have a sale on my seals and logos. I go about Facebook announcing the sale repeatedly, and I only allow a certain amount of people to take advantage of that sale within a certain time frame. For example, one of my most popular sales involved me letting the first ten customers take advantage a discounted logo design, and the sale was going to end in 24 hours. I would ask the customers to inbox me for more information about the sale because I didn't want to make the details of the sale public. I didn't want those details public because they could potentially hurt future sales. Anyhow, it never fails; in EVERY ONE of those sales, rebellion rears its ugly head. A couple of souls would inbox me for details, and I would send them the details and the rules; making sure to mention that the sale ends in 24 hours. After this, they would give me their email addresses so that I could invoice them. I would send them the invoice and continue on.

The following day, I would see that they hadn't paid the invoice yet. That's no problem. I'd advertise some more and be sure to post up that all unpaid invoices would be canceled at 12 am that night. I would receive no response from them, but I didn't expect one. I already knew what they were going to do before they did it because I knew I was dealing with the spirit of rebellion. They would wait until after 12 am and try to test me after I'd canceled their invoice. Each time, they'd tell me some dramatic story or claim that they didn't see the invoice. They'd ask me to resend the invoice. One time, I actually did resend an invoice to a woman and found that invoice the very next day still sitting unpaid. After I canceled it again, she emailed me again.

Please understand what these souls were doing. People will get you to go against your business by getting you to contend with, bend, or break your own rules. You may not realize it, but submitting to rebellion is basically spiritual espionage. You have betrayed the gift that GOD has given you for a few bucks just like Judas Iscariot betrayed JESUS for 30 shekels of silver.

Imagine that you worked as security for a large hotel. You had to stand at the door and make sure that everyone came in properly clothed and orderly. You were told by your boss not to let in anyone who is not wearing a shirt or shoes. They've drilled this in you over and over again, and you comply. Some man comes to the hotel's door one day, and he's not wearing a shirt or shoes. You politely explain to him that he cannot enter the hotel because he is not dressed appropriately. You run down the hotel's rules to him, but he doesn't want to hear them. Instead, he begins to berate you and demand that your manager be called. You pick up your walkee talkee and call a manager to the door. You're smiling and confident because your manager will see that you are doing your job, and he'll probably reward you for it.

Nevertheless, when the manager arrives, he listens to this irrational customer. You watch in horror as he agrees with the customer, promises to "take care" of you, and lets the customer in. In addition, he even offers the customer a free night because of his negative experience. How angry would you be?

Giving in to rebellion works the same way. Your rules are there to protect you, and your rules were set in place by GOD to keep your business running smoothly. But as soon as rebellion shows up with offense, you are ready to go against your own rules for the sake of pacifying some mouthy character? Don't do it. Instead, politely and firmly stand by your rules.

Use discernment with your customers. If the error was yours, correct it. If it is not a correction, it is a revision. Bill the customer accordingly and keep your business afloat.

Patience University

One of the most common issues that I have found when I mentored people in the past was patience. On average, most people that I have come across would give up on their business or business idea in as little as a month, and the most patient ones would hold out for a year. After they haven't seen any gain or progress in their business, they give up on it and go back to work in the secular world. Then, there are the ones that simply start a new business with a new idea and the cycle continues. They saw someone else making good money in a certain field, so they decide to go out there and hold out their net. After realizing that they haven't netted much, they continue this faithless cycle of chasing somebody else's tail looking for success.

Think about a college student. No student goes to college thinking that they will be bringing home a paycheck. Instead, they go to college with the understanding that they are going there to learn, and four to eight years later (depending on their major), they will be able to take what they've learned and start their career. However, people starting their own businesses often don't realize that there is a time when all they'll be doing is sowing and preparing for a harvest months or years later. As a result, many of them start and end businesses until they get frustrated and go back to school. Now, some of you may be saying, "Well, going back to school is a great idea, and it's good that they took this step towards their future." You're right, but consider this as well: The time they spent learning at a university is time they could have spent learning in the comfort of their own home. Let's be real here. This is the age of technology, where a person can learn just as much, if not more, from home at a computer than they could learn at a university. And let's not forget the price of learning from home, which, of course is free (if you don't count the monthly internet bill). What's the difference? Colleges often give out degrees where one can go into someone else's business and ask to get a job. Some majors even give you a few of the tools that you'll need to start your own business, but learning in your own spare time teaches you what you specifically need to know about your business type, the profit margins, the common errors, and so on. I'm not knocking school here because school can be a great resource of knowledge for some, but what I am saying is you have to train your mind to consider your time at home in front of a computer as your own personal college. The problem is the familiarity of the home setting and accountability. A lot of people go to school simply because they need to be accountable to someone else in order for them to stay consistent. I truly understand this, but this is an issue of self-control. This is where you have to step in and overcome yourself since you are your greatest hindrance. How can you overcome the familiarity and lazying comfort of being at home? Sometimes, it's as simple as removing familiarity from the picture, and other times, it is as difficult as training yourself to not give in to your own selfish desires to just lounge around.

Take yourself to an imaginary place called Patience University and make it your reality. Commit at least 30 minutes a day to your craft. Learn something new and do something new. It is better to do this at a set time every day to avoid slowly breaking the stride of things. You can start off working 30 minutes a day, six days a week, but this is to increase as you gain more knowledge. Study businesses like yours to see the going rates and the additional services you'll need to offer, and review the contracts if they are posted. The contracts will often tell you a lot about what common issues arise in that type of business. Take notes and study them.

Please note that faith and patience go hand in hand. You can't have one without the other. Don't be in a rush to launch out there. This is another reason a lot of Christian businesses close. The owner starts bubbling over with excitement, becomes anxious, and then just launches out there with little to no rules, no budget, and no plan. They just saw dollar signs. I've had a few friends to crash and burn their businesses like that. One day, they are excited about an idea that they said the LORD gave them, and they launch on out there. A few months later, they've closed that business and are onto something else. A year later, they've gone through several business ideas and have started working for other people with ideas. Lastly, they get excited about the other people's ideas and decide that they've gathered enough knowledge to start a business doing what they learned from someone else. A few months to a year later, they are back working in secular America, planning their next emotional business heist.

It takes an average two years to successfully launch a business and turn a decent profit, but the average American expects to be rich within a few months. In many cases, you won't see any business the first three to six months. This does not mean that your business is a bad idea; it could mean that you aren't doing something right. Maybe you're not advertising, or you're advertising to the wrong market.

Also, the first year or more, many business owners find themselves spending more than they are bringing in. This is a move of faith, but many don't see it that way. You are simply establishing your business and fortifying your business. It's how you view things that will determine how easily you give up or how patiently you stay in. You need the knowledge that all of your sister companies have, plus more. People will pay more money to go to a knowledgeable company than they would to go to a cheaper version of that company. You don't want to walk in anyone's shadow picking up the scraps that they drop.

Patience isn't easy to come by, because you have to be patient with patience. Patience is a virtue that you will have to pray for and believe GOD for. Then, there are the works that have to be put into place. This is where you'll have to take yourself through a school-like training and endure the pangs of wanting to do something else. There will be days when your favorite show comes on and you'll want to grab a bite to eat and watch the show. This is okay sometimes, but dedication always proves to be a gold-mine. You will find that the most successful people are the ones who learned to overcome selfish desires by making sacrifices, whereas many people who don't do well or that eventually close their businesses simply refused to make those sacrifices.

If GOD gives you a great idea, you have to be loyal to the idea, and it is always good to be loyal to GOD and make good on what HE has given you. If you said that HE gave you the idea, then why stop doing it? Take a look at the list below and apply these areas to your business. We'll call these Patience University courses.
1. Dedicate at least 30 minutes a day to your business; 5-6 days a week for the first three months. After three months, dedicate at least an hour a day to your business.
2. For the first year, write at least two rules a day to protect your business.
3. Every week, you need to purchase something that will benefit your business. Get what you can afford, but don't be cheap. When we spend enough to get our own attention, we are less likely to give up on the business because of the investments we put into it. This is you telling you that you're serious about what GOD gave you.
4. Add a new service to your business once a week for the first

year, even if your sister companies don't offer this service. The idea is growth. Anything that does not grow is lifeless. Sometimes, you will find that what gives your business the edge is the fact that you are offering an array of services that your sister companies don't offer. The goal is to become a major player and not just a little dot on a large map.

5. Ask questions and set up conferences. One reason people lose interest in their own ideas is because they weren't too involved in them in the first place. You have to court and date your ideas often to keep that spark going.

6. Buy some inexpensive notepads and carry them around with you. The LORD will often give you ideas or minister to you in some peculiar places because HE is a peculiar GOD. It is better to be equipped to write down those ideas than to risk forgetting them.

7. Start a business account and deposit a little money into it every now and again. Do not touch this money! Even if you can only afford to put $5 a week in this account, it will serve as a reminder to you that you are a business owner and that you have some great things in the making.

You can apply those ideas to help yourself get over the hump of long-suffering. Remember these pointers for a successful business start-up and continuation:

1. Hold your horses. Don't run out and try to hire people just yet. You need to learn the ins and outs of the business, the laws of your state, and the federal laws regarding employment before you venture out to hire people. Sometimes we get so excited about the big picture that we try to create it in haste. This is error. If you're a woman, imagine looking at some model on television whose makeup looks flawless. Now, hastily try to do that to your face and see what it looks like. You may be able to put makeup on pretty fast, but perfection takes time.

2. If you feel overwhelmed, back away from the workspace and take a breather. Anything we have to force ourselves to do, we begin to hate; but anything we will ourselves to do becomes a passion. This is why you have to absolutely convince yourself that it will work. If you're unsure, you'll pull away eventually

and chase after someone else's dreams. Sometimes, taking a break or a day off is what you need to collect yourself, but don't take days off often, or you'll get used to running when the business steps on your toes. I would venture to say that you are to only take days off when it is absolutely necessary, but don't take days off because you don't feel like studying or working.

3. If you find yourself not having patience with your craft, maybe it isn't your gifting but your attempt at chasing the dreams of someone else. When it is a gift, we will have a passion for it, but when it is a job or an attempt to earn money, we will grow impatient with it. This is human nature. Your gifts will make room for you and bring you before great men. Not the gifts or talents of someone else.

4. Take your time and do it right. The worst type of business owner is an anxious one.

Just remember that you're not the first person who has battled with patience, if this is your struggle. You can, however, become a rare success story by overcoming the battle with impatience. Successful people often become successful after refusing to back down to fear and refusing to give up on GOD.

<u>Assassinating Familiarity</u>

Why are we choosing to "assassinate" familiarity? The word "assassinate" means to kill a high-ranking individual, usually for religious or political reasons. Familiarity ranks high in the lives of most people until they are delivered from it. We learn to depend on and follow the rules of familiarity just so that we can make it through each day without being shunned or overtaken by the unknown. This is a faith walk, not a fake walk

Here are a few things that you can do to refresh your home and make it into a comfortable place to do business:
1. Rearrange your office area or create an office area in a room in your house. Remember this: If your area is crowded and junky, it will serve more as a prison cell than as an office. Some people say that they work better in the familiar ruins of junk, but how we live on the outside bears witness to what's going on inside of us. If your heart is a mess, you will feel comfortable in the midst of junk. In that case, it is always better to do a self analysis and send up a prayer to Heaven before proceeding with starting a business. Business failure, in the majority of cases, has everything to do with the business owner.

2. Remove distractions from your office space. You know what serves as a distraction to you. It is that very thing (or things) that bothers your conscious or sub-conscious mind. For example, I don't like open doors behind me. I'm not afraid of someone coming through those doors, but I just don't like them open, so I close all doors behind me and get to work. Another common distraction is a television set. Some people proudly put a television set in their office and wonder why they can't work at certain times. Familiarity reminds them that their favorite soap opera is on or their favorite show is about to come on, and even when they decide to work instead of watch television, they are often distracted by their thoughts. That is to say, don't put a television or other distraction in your office setting.

3. Don't place your office in a distracting area. There goes that television set again. Some people place their offices where they can view the TV from another room, and then they wonder why they can't get much done. Some place their office too close to the kitchen and then eventually close their businesses, citing that they gained weight while sitting and working from home. They feel that the healthier choice or line of work for them is to work somewhere else. So basically, people don't own businesses or continue owning businesses because they can't trust themselves to do right. This has to change if you expect and desire for the business to have staying power.

4. Set a schedule to work during the time where you'd usually be asleep, chatting, or eating. What you're doing is breaking down the walls of familiarity and repetition. These are the very strongholds that have closed so many businesses. You have to do something different to obtain different results. Some people, for example, eat at noon and then try to work. Thirty-minutes to an hour after eating, they find themselves drowsy. For example, I have found that I work better hungry. I eat after I have accomplished a certain amount of work. I take breaks during my drowsy periods to recollect myself, and if I haven't gotten a lot of sleep, I'll take a one-hour nap. These naps, for

me, are very rare because I'm usually able to fight it off by taking a break and advertising.

5. Post up long-term goal reminders and daily reminders around you. The long-term goal reminders should be moved around every couple of days to a week, since the human mind tends to get familiar with settings and begins to overlook everything that is familiar to it. The short-term goal reminders should be in a crate, for example, as goals that you have to accomplish on that particular day. You can also create a crate for weekly goals and accomplishments.

6. Let your friends go to voice mail. Sure, Vicky calls every day at a certain time, but it's usually because Vicky is not busy. It's okay to take breaks whenever you can and talk on the phone, but it is always better to be productive in your day and only make or take phone calls on your break. Even then, they need to be timed so you can get back to work.

7. Get out and exercise more. What a weird pointer, right? Exercise is not only good for the body, but it is even better for the mind. Exercise causes the body to reduce pheromones. Pheromones are nicknamed "the feel good hormones" for a reason. This will put you in a better mood and make it easier for you to work. Pay attention to a lot of successful office executives. They are usually in shape and happy.

8. Place a mirror on your desk. (Warning, don't do this if you're conceited or you'll only distract yourself, but you're saved, so I'm sure there's no one reading this book that's conceited.) Placing a mirror on your desk will sometimes help you to check yourself when your mood is off balance. You may be getting frustrated with a client over the phone, but when you turn and see yourself in the mirror, it may help you to calm down.

9. If you are working from home, dress like you are going in an office. It's amazing how the human mind works. When a person is dressed for bed, they'll end up heading towards the

bedroom. When someone is dressed to lounge around, they'll find their way to the couch. When someone is dressed to work, they'll usually go and work.

10. Take lunch breaks and take yourself out sometimes. You may have a mean chicken sandwich waiting for you in the fridge, but it is always good to change your scenery for an hour to unwind. You deserve it. Give yourself one to two hour lunch breaks and stick with your schedule.

11. Socialize with more people that are unlike you (in a good way). I have met foreigners who have been in America for decades, and their English is just as bad as the day they came here. I've also met foreigners who have been in America for a year or more whose English is far better than the ones that have been here for decades. What I found was that the ones who had bad English did not socialize with many Americans in their personal lives. They moved into communities where other people from their countries lived, and they communicated primarily with them. They went to work and didn't communicate too much with their co-workers; only speaking when it was necessary. The ones who spoke audible English usually had American friends that they frequently socialized with. The ones who chose not to communicate too much with Americans usually did this out of fear and/ or an unwillingness to adapt to the cultures of people unlike them.

You are a foreigner to a certain mindset, and you need to learn the language of success. You won't learn this language speaking to people who speak a language you recognize; you will learn this language listening to people who speak a language that you don't recognize. You won't learn the language of success hanging out with people that you can relate to; you'll learn this hanging around people that you want to relate to.

Exposing and Denouncing Procrastination

Procrastination was a stronghold that I battled with. It was a generational mindset that weighed me down and told me to stay where I was. It promised to release me soon, but that never happened. Instead, GOD released me from procrastination. It was a heaviness, and I always tried to pacify it by just giving in to it. The reward it gave me was relaxation in the body, but what it took from me was relaxation in my mind. I knew that I had much to do, and GOD had given me many ideas, but I just didn't feel like carrying them through. Each day I'd put my destiny off so that I could continue to enjoy time with myself and the lies the enemy told me. Everything was put off until tomorrow, next week, next month, or next year. One day I decided to pray procrastination off me. GOD is so faithful. When it came off, GOD made sure HE let me see that I was released. I went into overdrive with working what HE'D given me.

Today's a great day to start on that road towards your release. In starting and running a successful Christian business, you will find that there are many projects you have to complete one at a time. Sometimes, you may find yourself feeling anxious, and you'll want to try to tackle them all at once. As time goes on, you'll learn better and do better.

You'll know when you're under the siege of procrastination

when you find yourself putting things off and trying to reason with yourself and others as to why you're doing it. One of the ways to expose procrastination is to call it out and challenge it. You do this by setting up a list of things to do for a week. Don't try to take on the easier tasks, but jump right into the challenging duties. Dedicate 30 minutes to an hour of working towards your mark every day that week. Procrastination will make itself known when you are prepping for work in body, but your mind wants to do something else. Sometimes it's not procrastination, but repetition that has you in its grips. Procrastination, however, has a familiar behavior to it, whereas you won't necessarily want to fall into repetition; instead, you just don't want to do what you have scheduled yourself to do. If you get through the week without procrastination bothering you, then set a schedule for a month. If procrastination is there, it is sure to bother you then, since it is reported that a habit is broken within 17-21 days. You challenge procrastination by getting busy and proactively working towards your mark.

To denounce procrastination is to speak to it vocally and evict it from your heart, but that's not the end of it. First, have you ever met someone who told their boyfriend to get out of their house, but when you went to visit them again, he was still there? You'll find many people who do this with demonic strongholds. They tell it to get away from them, but they'll go back and reconcile with it when they find themselves missing the adrenaline rushes of stormy weather or the calming sounds of nothingness. The second part to denouncing something is actually denouncing and overcoming your desire to go back to it because it is like a break-up. You will often find yourself missing that familiar place of just being idle. No matter how terrible a place is, when we get used to it, we begin to actually grow fond of it. Remember what the Israelites did when GOD rescued them from the Egyptians? They complained and wished in their hearts that they'd never left their bondage. They actually missed being slaves to the Egyptians and they missed being mistreated. What about those slaves that were freed after the Civil War but chose not to leave their slave masters out of fear of the unknown? People do get comfortable in bondage, and trying to bring them out can be a blood-drawing challenge.

The first part of freeing yourself is freeing your mind before you free your body. If your mind is still in captivity, your body will soon follow. You have to actually force feed the mind new information because it will not want to willingly consume it. The mind does not like to be stretched. If you don't believe this, go to a school and see how many happy kids are in calculus class. You'll probably find one out of thirty students, and he or she would be the one considered strange or nerdy. In force feeding the mind, don't overdo it. Sometimes, we can try to take in so much information that we actually lose information. Know when your mind's been topped off for the day and start again tomorrow.

Another way to expose procrastination is to review how much work needs to be done to launch your business and compare it to how much you have actually done. Now, this is for those who have already launched out or began the launching process. You should have a list of things that need to be done, and every week, you need to see how much of it that you've actually done. Document how you felt before starting the work, during your time working, and after the completion of the work. This will help you to understand your own way of thinking and where you need the most work. This will also help you to tailor your prayer and send it up to Heaven. Sometimes, people pray for the wrong things. They pray for the healing of the surface, because it is what they can see, but they don't think to pray for the uprooting of whatever has caused that thing to surface. If I go outside and cut down a weed, it'll only grow back. I'll have to pull it up by the roots or use a chemical to kill the roots to keep it from growing back.

Be sure to pray and ask the LORD to deliver you from procrastination, and anytime you feel procrastination trying to seduce you, speak to it and tell it that it is not welcome. Bind it and cast it away from you. Then get up and do exactly what it was trying to stop you from doing. You're not only saying to procrastination that your relationship is over, but you are showing procrastination that you've started a whole new relationship and there is just no room for it anymore.

Fear of Success

This is a real condition characterized by excessive excuse making and running away from one's own gifts. Believe it or not, this is a common reason for people to thrust themselves back into secular jobs and into the arms of familiarity. People sometimes fear what they could become or have because they don't know what's going to happen from there. And when you begin to scratch the surface of success, you will start to experience many changes in your personal life that aren't always pleasant or welcome. For example, your friends may become your enemies; not because you've done something wrong to them, but because they don't recognize or like the changes that GOD has made or is making in you. Sometimes envy enters the equation. People can deal with you when you are on their level, but once GOD elevates you, they won't know how to deal with the changed you. For example, your best buddy may see people who make a certain amount of income or talk a certain way as arrogant. This is because he or she has never made that amount of income, and they socialize with people who speak a certain way, and these are the people that they can identify with. Let's say that you start making that kind of income and speaking properly to better communicate with your customers, and this becomes habit. Now, you're on the wrong side of their radar because you are no longer the you that they know. You are a different character; you are changed.

Your friends have to be like spandex; able to fit you not matter what size you get, and the only type of friends who can do this are friends who themselves have stretchmarks. They don't have to be successful; they can be just as poor as or poorer than you in finances, but they cannot be poorer than you in faith.

Many who begin to experience these changes run back to be their old familiar self whom everyone knows and loves. They choose to close down their businesses, or they let the devil suck the wind out of their businesses, so they can maintain these relationships. Why didn't they just love the people enough to let them go? After all, in growing, GOD may sometimes bring them back around to you to see what HE has done for you in their absence. This isn't to rub it in their faces, but it is to glorify HIS Name and show them what HE can do for them. This is why your success is important. You aren't just being successful for you, but there are others who will learn to believe GOD because of what HE does for you.

Then, there are the souls that get to a certain place in success and begin to unpack their fears there. They don't want to go any further because things have gotten too weird and unpredictable from where they are. As your business grows, you should be investing more money and time into the business as well as earning more. In most cases, when people reach this height, they often continue investing the same amount of time and money that they've been investing for months or years. This doesn't grow the business; it maintains the business. This is the place that they've chosen as their comfort zone in fear because here, they are able to maintain those relationships that they've acquired along the way or those old familiar relationships that were threatened by their success.

Fear is real and fear of success is a reality for many. It's funny how people make vows not to change to those that they fear they'll lose along the way. Change is inevitable when we are elevated into success because success is not just financially founded. Success is also having an abundance of knowledge and knowing where and how to apply that knowledge. The final touch is actually applying that knowledge (the works) with the expectation of results (faith), be they minor or major.

Take a look around you. What are you afraid of losing? Men often fear success because they are afraid of the changes that will occur during the process, and women often fear losing the loving relationship that they have with their husbands; so they get to a certain place in their business and park there. Mothers oftentimes fear what success would do to their children or what success would expose their children to. After all, you'd probably have to move into an area where the way of thinking is different than what you're accustomed to. Fear not. During your transition, the LORD will change your mind as you gradually take each step towards your predestined height in HIM. Relationships that were seasonal will shed their leaves and wither away, and you'll eventually learn to stop apologizing for being blessed.

The ultimate goal shouldn't be to acquire riches for yourself, but your aim should be to glorify GOD and help others to reach their potential in HIM. You can never help a man reach the top when you're living at the bottom. In addition, your children need to know that they can be all that GOD has called them to be, and they don't have to be afraid to be blessed. I asked myself one day what was my ultimate goal with the businesses, books, and all that GOD has me doing. I felt really good with the answer that surfaced: My goal is to successfully be everything that GOD has called me to be in HIM, without apology. To leave a legacy that glorifies HIM and helps others to understand that GOD is real and HE is able to do above all that we can ever ask or think. I'm done with procrastination, and I've ended my relationship with fear. Now, I want to make my FATHER proud in every way possible. I thought of the financial success, and it didn't really move me. I found myself glowing at the thought of being able to be a blessing to others. This is true success; to have the heart and love that FATHER has HIMSELF instilled in you. I too had to learn to stop fearing success. I didn't even realize that I was afraid of it until I saw it coming up the mountain and it looked intimidating. I saw friends walking away from me and family pulling away, and I wanted to go back to that state of relaxation in familiarity, but more than that, I did not want to disappoint GOD. So, I chose to stay in HIS will and embrace the unknown, knowing that HE will not let my foot dash against a rock.

Fear is simply a small hill that looks like a mountain from where you are standing. You can choose to retreat and go back to your familiar place or you can continue on towards that mirage of a mountain. When you finally stare fear in the face, faith will cause it to shrink and show its true form, and you can easily step across it. Yes, you will be shunned; even by "church-folks," but this doesn't mean that what you are doing is wicked. Sometimes it means that what you are doing is exposing the wickedness in them, or they can be good people who don't understand your walk because they have never worn your shoes. People often critique what they don't recognize, but this is not your problem unless you make it your problem. Your focus is to remain and has to remain on CHRIST, or you'll get sucked in to somebody's definition of you and never reach your full potential. You'll be all they expected you to be but nowhere near what GOD called you to be and of course, this is a sin and a shame. When you don't answer the calling on your life, like Jonah, you will have a whale of problems waiting for you.

Fear also shrinks the vision and makes it appear small enough for us to feel comfortable with it. For example, you may envision yourself in a modest house with a small business and manageable monthly payments to your mortgage company, business building, and car note. Imagining yourself in the house of your dreams with a huge successful business and no debt is a stretch of faith. Just because you are comfortable with the idea of "small" doesn't mean that you should remain comfortable in this mindset. Instead, when you find yourself with walled-in faith, you should be praying and beating down those walls. This is something that should not be put off, but should be executed immediately. Test yourself to see how high your faith can jump. Browse the internet and find an available home that is everything you want and more, and ask yourself if you can ever have this home. If your answer is negative or unsure, then you've found the walls of your faith. Faith should always be without walls since we serve the CREATOR of all things. Fear simply means you need more WORD in you.

There are the ones who have convinced themselves that their vision is modest and they pursue these dreams by tip-toeing towards them, hoping that they don't get up and run away. After reaching the peak of their modesty and accomplishing what they have set out to accomplish, they find themselves unsatisfied with their lives, so they set new goals that look to be within reach of their faith. For example, if their goal to earn $100,000 a year was accomplished, they may feel comfortable shooting for $150,000 a year. Nevertheless, tell them that they can earn $500,000 a year, and the smoke of offense will arise to reveal the walls of fear that has imprisoned them. Some people simply take baby steps in faith, and this is okay when you're a baby, but as you grow up in HIM, you have to learn to take giant leaps that make others question your sanity.

We often hear leaders ask that daring question, "What will you believe GOD for?" The word "will" means to give permission to or voluntarily make yourself available to. A good question to ask yourself is, "What have you been believing fear for?" This is to help you to see the reflection of where you really are so that you can shatter that familiar mirror and walk into the discomforting place of trusting GOD until it becomes comfortable for you. You should never wait for fear to challenge you before you take it on. Sometimes, you have to go looking for fear, call it out, and challenge it with your faith.

<u>Why Many Christian Businesses Fail</u>

A lot of Christians are afraid to label their business as a Christian business. Many refuse to run their business as a Christian business because they want to avoid both the stigma and the challenges of trying to stay afloat in a secular world. You can run, operate, and have a successful Christian business without compromising your beliefs and morals. The number one thing to remember is to trust GOD, and number two is to not chase money. Your reason for having a Christian business should not be the same reason a man of the world has a business. His goal is to earn money and obtain power, but your focus should be on glorifying and obeying GOD. I know that's hard to digest considering you do want to earn money in what you do, but you have to remember Matthew 6:33: *"But seek ye first the kingdom of God, and his righteousness; and all these things shall be added unto you."* The funny thing about a Christian business is that you won't just be a Christian business owner, but you are commanded to win souls. I understand that if you have a coffee shop, you wouldn't be able to walk around the shop ministering to others, but sometimes GOD will allow the opportunity to present itself to you. You have to absolutely change your focal point so that you can go after what GOD has called you to come after. Chasing dollar signs always leads you into dark places.

Here are 11 reasons why most Christian businesses fail:

1. Anxious leadership. Sometimes, the owner is so anxious that he or she does not do all of the necessary legal work to protect their business. In addition, sometimes this anxiousness will cause them to jump out of the boat before they've learned to swim. You have to stay calm and remember that every season has a reason. Take each step one foot at a time.

2. Procrastination. I'll do this tomorrow, and I'll do that next week. Procrastination is a stronghold that imprisons the mind of a person. Their desires are to serve their "feelings" rather than contend with them.

3. Being cheap. I have found that more than fifty percent of Christian business owners are, for lack of a better term, cheap. Their branding looks horrible, and their presentation is humiliating to the Kingdom. You may be saying, "Well, they may not have a lot of money right now." Most of the people that I have come in contact with in my dealings actually do have enough to brand themselves the right way. The problem is that they are still counting money and not counting blessings. They simply have a preference as to what they want to do with their money, and oftentimes, they don't take ministry seriously enough to actually spend on it. Go to their houses, and you'll find an elaborately designed space that looks like it's fit for a king. Go to their churches, and you'll find a run-down building that looks like it's fit for a prisoner. When it comes to all things Christian, some people just haven't arrived at the wholeness or understanding of who GOD is just yet. They are still trying to reach to the bottom of their purses and give GOD their loose change, but when it comes to themselves, their families, and everything else; they'll pay handsomely. This is an indication

as to how they view GOD and what HE has given them. A business that looks like a run-down mom and pop business will get customers who have learned how to negotiate down a mom and pop business. They won't deal with that business the same way they'd deal with a large business that's fortified by rules. In addition, people who are faithful customers that don't have a wrongful relationship with money will steer away from such businesses. Instead, they'll prefer to pay a more expensive, well-established business because it looks like a business and presents itself like a business.

4. Hiring familiar folks. This is a gun that's almost always sure to backfire. If you want to hear about the effects of this, interview some successful business owners and some non-successful business owners and compare the interviews. They'll share some funny stories with you about hiring familiar faces. Some of the successful ones actually did this at some point and found how much it held their business back, and some of the not so successful businesses are still doing this and may not recognize how it is affecting their business. If it's going to be, for example, a family-run business, that's okay. A family-run business is usually run by a father, mother and their children; not uncles, aunts, nieces, nephews, and cousins. Someone I know told me that they'd hired people from their church, and this caused a backlash because, not surprisingly, the people didn't want to treat it like it was a job. Instead, they saw it as their church member's business, and they felt like they didn't have to work as hard as they would have to do in a large company; they felt like they didn't have to be dependable, and they felt like the business owner had to abide by their rules. If they didn't, they would have to deal with that person's backlash, which included, but was not limited to: talking to the leader of that church about them, not speaking to the business owner, and lastly, spreading rumors about the owner. People who don't know you will usually take your business a lot more seriously and work a lot harder than someone who knows you. When you first launch out, of course, you're going to want your relatives, friends, and family to jump in and give you a hand.

The problem is....they are familiar with you. As a result, they won't work as hard as someone who is not familiar, they won't come to work as often as they should, and they won't take any delegation from you because you're you! In addition, this setup often leads to strained personal relationships as well as critically injured businesses.

5. Not setting rules or not abiding by the rules they set. Too many businesses out there don't have any rules in place, and the ones that do have a few set up, don't require their customers to honor those rules. Your rules are for your protection and your customer's protection and understanding. Rules help you to create and run a peaceful business, whereas a lack of rules opens your doors up for chaos and unruliness to enter. Be sure to set rules. Every time you come in contact with a customer that overworks you, put a new rule in place immediately to protect yourself from this happening again. For every problem you face, you should write a new rule and publish it to your site and your manual. In addition, you're going to get customers that simply do not want to abide by your rules; that's a given. I come in contact with them pretty often, but not as often as I used to. I've learned how to handle such customers in a professional way where we don't end up going back and forward. What I do is refer them to my already published rules and send them to forms that require additional payment for additional services. Some will happily comply with the rules or pay, and others will complain. No one said business ownership would be easy. Additionally, you will have the customers that claim that they didn't know a particular rule was in existence. This is why you need to make sure your rules are published where the customer can see them and have your customers sign contracts where the rules are published so that they can be referred back to those contracts. For me, it does not matter if the customer chose to or chose not to read the rules; rules are rules and everyone has to abide by them. When a customer is contentious and continues to say that they didn't know a rule was in existence, what they are really saying is, "I don't want to abide by that rule, and I shouldn't have to

because I didn't read it." If you were traveling down the highway going 85 miles per hour in a 55 mile per hour zone and the police pulled you over, do you think that they'd excuse you because you chose not to read the posted speed signs? Of course not. I don't say this to my customers, but this example helps me to firmly glue myself in a stable "no" when they request that I overlook my own rules. In addition, one of the mottoes on my site and on my rules page in bold lettering is, "Not reading the rules does not make you exempt from them." The reason you have to stay grounded and honor your own rules is because your business will begin to acquire a reputation, and you don't want others to say, "Hey, you can talk him down. Just argue with him for a while and he'll give in." People actually do this! It is better to lose a customer that does not want to abide by your rules than to have people treat your business like a broken vending machine.

6. Disorder. No one wants to do business with a disorderly business. If you went to see your doctor and she had your files mixed in with other folks' files, you'd probably be scared and run for safety. When someone calls you or visits your location, they love it when you can get straight to their file and you give them the answer that they need. A computer system (with backup) is a great way to organize your files. You can also print those files and keep them in a filing cabinet for safe keeping.

7. No vision and no plans. If you have ever gone into a business where there was obviously no vision and no plans, you would see it from the door. The business owner may always seem aggressive and agitated and may try to do all things his or herself. The phone is ringing off the hook, and the owner is struggling to handle you and the customers in line. The owner simply shows up at the building every day remembering their role in running the business, but they seem to have forgotten that they need to keep the business running. Someone with no vision will jump around to everything. You may go into a barber shop and find that they are selling produce on the other side. You'll leave there with a haircut and a bag of oranges.

They are just going with the monetary flow and trying to find a way to stay afloat.

When a military goes into war, it has to have a strategy. They have plan A, plan B, and so on. They don't just show up to war as if they are cashiers; they have to be proactive in staying alive and accomplishing their mission. You should do the same with your business. Showing up isn't enough, but you have to have a plan. You should also have a plan for expansion. You can develop your expansion plan once a month.

8. Not operating in their called places. You can't run a business that was not for you in the first place. It is always error to try to find your place in someone else's anointing.

9. Disloyal leadership. In mentoring, I have helped a few people to start up their businesses (glory to GOD), but I can't help to keep them afloat. What I've found is that a lot of people don't stay loyal to the vision. They grow impatient and decide that they are better off in another field of business. One day, they launch a business selling shoes, and the next month, they've decided to close their shoe business and start painting walls. It is very rare for a person to start a business and garner immediate success. You have to stay dedicated to the vision even when you can't see it. On average, it takes two years of consistently running, investing in, and upgrading a business before one can expect to earn a full time income from their business or get back what they've put into it. If you're not that patient, then business ownership is not for you just yet.

10. No advertising or little advertising. This usually goes under the "cheap" category, but it deserves its own platform. How do you expect someone to know about your business if you don't advertise it?

11. Not trusting GOD and not being loyal to GOD. When you labeled that business a Christian business, you were saying that this business honors the LORD, JESUS CHRIST. Now, you've got

to demonstrate it and be loyal to GOD with your business even when hard times are upon you. If CHRIST is the head of your business, then the body of your business must move in sync with HIM. If it doesn't, HE'S not the head of it. All too often, people place fear, impatience, and a love for money as the head of their businesses. For a while, they seem to be going somewhere because these sins project a false sense of success or a false sense of inching towards success. If you don't trust a man, you wouldn't follow him down a road; would you? If you don't trust GOD, you won't follow HIM as well. Disloyalty to GOD is always a sign that you don't trust HIM or that you trust more in yourself, your devices, your money, your fears, and/ or others. This way of thinking always digs a graveyard for a Christian business because, again, when you claim the name, you need to represent the name well. When you don't trust GOD, you will always make a deal with the devil..........guaranteed.

Hiring Devils for Protection

Have you ever seen a Christian hanging out with a demon-filled soul? They claim to be trying to win the soul, but instead of ministering to them, they are hanging out with them. They turn around and hire this person to work for them, and they seem to favor this person over all their employees. What's going on with them, and why don't they lift up their sisters and brothers in CHRIST? The answer is simple. People think they need to hire devils to deal with devils.

I've seen this one too many times. Someone who just wants to deal with the business end of things, without having to deal with confrontational customers ends up hiring someone who is confrontational to deal with such customers. They tend to favor these souls because they admire the lack of fear and protective nature of these souls. In a sense, they feel protected when these characters are around, and they feel that they can focus on the business at hand when these characters are present.

You may be saying that you can handle your own customers, no matter how antagonistic they are, but not everyone likes confrontation. All the same, as a Christian business owner, you have to be careful how you handle people because you don't want to misrepresent CHRIST. As Christians, many of us try to deal with each customer on their level because we feel that a bully only understands flesh, and a sweet soul must be handled with care.

When I started out, I tried to stay away from arguing with my customers. I just wanted to do the work I was hired to do and present an excellent piece to my client. In my imagination, the client would be overjoyed, and we'd continue working together as time passed. In most cases, I got what I wanted; but in some cases, I had to deal with aggressive and manipulative people who tried to use their aggression as their guns. In other words, people will try to rob you with their attitudes. When I didn't have a lot of rules, I got plenty of aggressive customers, and I end up getting in the flesh with them because I was still battling with that flesh. Needless to say, I was a poor Kingdom representative, but I was dying daily. As time passed, GOD taught me that I kept getting aggressive customers because I didn't have any rules in place, or any rules published. I was just flying along like a kite, and hoping for the best. It never failed; I would always eventually get someone who would try to get over on me and then snarl like that was going to make me submit. Could hiring a person like them help me? No. Let me explain.

Each time that you are exposed to a troubling customer, GOD is giving you a new rule to put in place. This person comes along and exposes your company's weaknesses or the weaknesses in your rules. What should you do with these types of people? Don't work with them. Explain your rules, and refer them to your rules. If you don't have a rule in place, since you are the business owner, you have the following options:
- Immediately put one in place and enforce it. Of course, this would make the customer upset, but who cares? Believe me; it doesn't matter what you do, they are going to snarl because that's what devils do.

- Go ahead and extend yourself this time, and put a rule in place so that this doesn't happen again. Be sure to let the customer know that this is the only and the last time that you can extend yourself to help them. If you don't, they'll come back looking to take advantage of you.
- Give the customer an option to receive a full refund, or to go by your verbal rules. You can basically tell a customer what you will and will not allow.

Hiring devils to deal with devils always backfires. What a man is and what a man has is deeply embedded in his being, and he won't change his ways just because you are nice to him. Take a zebra and dip it in water, and you will see that it does not lose its stripes. Just the same, a person doesn't go through deliverance just because you are being nice to them.

When you hire a person because they are undelivered in an area, that area where they need deliverance is going to be the very area that they attack you from. In addition, other areas where they are in bondage will begin to show up as you are being bound. For example, let's say that you opened a business in a bad neighborhood and you hired a man that was common to that area. You feel safe with him in your business because he knows just about everyone in the area, and many people fear him. He's intimidating, but he needs financial help, so you see this as a worthy tradeoff. That is until he begins to intimidate you. Souls that are undelivered can sense your fears, and they will prey on them. Try firing them for not doing their job, and they will become the very person you were trying to protect yourself from.

There were several cases where a business owner had hired a lost soul hoping to be a blessing to them, and at the same time, use their demons to guard their business. Instead of protecting the business, the person began stealing from the company. When the owner found out that they were being robbed, they fired them and paid for their decision with their life. The ones who were not killed were often harassed, intimidated, or stalked by the very people they once tried to use.

Your role with such souls is to usher them towards GOD, not use them. How can a person appreciate what you do for them if they don't appreciate what GOD does for them? How can a person that dishonors GOD honor you? How can a person who is not loyal to GOD be loyal to you? First things first; they need deliverance and secondly, GOD is your protector. In addition, HE will give you a set of rules to protect your business, but you have to write them out, publish them, and enforce them.

How should you deal with aggressive customers?
- Point them to your rules.
- Before you proceed, make sure that you are right and they are wrong. After that, stand by your rules.
- Be polite, but firm. Your rules are your rules.
- Do not give in "this time" or any other time to their demands just because they are persistently and aggressively coming after you. This is what they do, and this works in the world, but it should not work with you.
- If you haven't provided a service or a product to them just yet, go ahead and refund them and then ban them from ever doing business with you. Remember, do this politely and professionally.
- If you have provided them with a service or a product, but they are trying to get more, simply stand by your rules and utilize your phone's features: the disconnect button, caller identification screen, and call block.
- If necessary, report them to the proper authorities.
- Don't listen to them reason with you over and over again because they are only going to say the same thing a different way. Aggressive people have learned that aggression can be used as a weapon to get what they want. Don't feed into that ignorance. Instead of listening to them go on and on about what they want, stop answering their calls.
- Never change your number to get away from an aggressive customer. They will only find it and continue

to harass you. Instead, stand your ground and mean what you say. Eventually, they'll get it and go away.

To prevent getting such a customer, use discernment. I have had potential customers to call me and question me about my services and I could hear that devil on them. I knew that they would be no joke to work with. A few of them have even admittedly given their last designer a hard time because the designer basically didn't comply to their demands. What I do is refer them to my site's rules and make it clear that I don't bend them. If their issue with the other designer is an issue that I know they'd have with me, I defend the other designer and explain to them why this rule is in place. In 100% of these situations, the customer did not hire me; thank GOD. To them, their money is temptation, but GOD gave me a way of escape and I took it by informing them of my rules beforehand. I was professional and I was nice, and I was informative. Most people that are aggressive tend to talk with you a little longer than most customers because they are looking for a way around your rules. Once they realize that you won't bend, in most cases, they won't work with you. That's not a bad thing! Because they will cost you more than they pay you.

Remember, a zebra does not lose its stripes just because you pour water on it. Hire whomever GOD tells you to hire because they have been trained by GOD, and equipped by GOD to be just what you need. When a soul needs deliverance, tell them about JESUS CHRIST. You will only confuse them by telling them about their ways, and then exploiting those very same ways. At the same time, you will fall under judgment the minute you cause one of GOD'S little ones (babies and babes in CHRIST) to stumble.

Partnerships, Affiliates and Networking

Partnerships
When you hear someone offer to partner with you, they are either offering:
a. To send customers to you (and vice-versa). They have their own business, you have your own business, but they are asking to help you while you help them. This is good if you are offering a service that ties into what they are offering. For example, if you create flyers, then it would be good to partner with a printing company.
b. To give you a recurring monetary gift to help keep your business running, or they may be asking you to give them a recurring monetary gift to help keep their business running. Sometimes they may offer to give away their services or products freely, or they may be asking you to give away your services or products freely. You would need to decide if it's worth it or not.
c. To go into business with you. This means the two of you will share ownership of the same business. This is always a no-no if GOD didn't tell you to do so. This always seems like a good idea

when you need some help, but once those contracts are signed, there is no turning back.

Personally, I think the best way to do a partnership is for someone to have their own business, and you should have your own business. You could agree to offer their services from your company at a raised rate and give them their required fee and allow them to do the same for you. The reason it's not good to directly send your customers to them is because they may decide to offer the very same services that you are offering. In business, there aren't too many nice guys. Just because you have morals and limitations doesn't mean the next guy has them.

In addition, please educate yourself on the laws and lawsuits affiliated with partnerships. Never partner with anyone who does not have as much as you, since they stand to gain, whereas you stand to lose. In addition, never partner with anyone who isn't as dedicated to their vision as you are to yours.

Affiliates

Affiliates are just the businesses that you affiliate with. Oftentimes, these are the companies that ask you to place their link on your site or their signs in your store and in return, they promise to do this for you. Link exchange can be good for S.E.O. (search engine optimization), but affiliate linking has its advantages and disadvantages. Again, it is not uncommon for a business that you link up with to start selling the very same products and services that you are selling. If they believe it to be a good market to get into, they will go there, and they don't need your permission to do so. Affiliate linking is only good, in my opinion, when you're trading links or when you absolutely know and trust the affiliate. I speak from experience when I say: Many, if not most, of the people that linked up to me tried to jump into one or more of the markets that I am in. So I couldn't affiliate with them business-wise because this would be a poor marketing choice for my business. You have to understand that most people that try to link up with you as a business or as a friend who came through the knowledge of your business are looking to see how your business can help theirs.

Affiliate marketing is good because you'll likely deal with larger companies that allow you to place their links on your site, and they'll pay you for it. Or they'll allow you to sell their products and get a commission. You won't find too many large companies that will sell your products; however, and when you do, their rates are usually expensive.

Networking
Networking is still a form of affiliate marketing, but it can be defined differently by each business. In networking, the business owners have agreed to come together and find ways to help one another. They may agree to periodic business meetings, shared documentations, and so on. But whenever someone says that they want to network with you, it is always good to ask for their definition of networking. Some people simply mean they want to share ideas, or better yet, bleed you of your ideas; but I digress. Some people mean they want to partner with you, and others mean that they want to create or add you to an existing network of people who help one another by providing each other resources, ideas and by exchanging links.

In all things, be prayerful. I used to jump at every idea that sounded like a good idea until I stopped chasing money and learned that my success would only come from GOD. In all that jumping around, partnering, and so on; I have found that the best thing you can do is partner with GOD, affiliate with GOD, and network with GOD. Sometimes it sounds like a great idea to link up with other businesses, but that's only when you get stirred up emotionally. Once you take the time to pray on it and think about it, you'll usually come back with a different answer and a different way of seeing it.

The closer you get to success, the more people you will find that try to link up to you. They aren't necessarily bad people, but sometimes they are just desperate and looking for a way to skip the process. People usually believe that you are or can be their key to success. One of the most common things you'll hear people say is that they've got a great idea that can benefit your business and it'll make the two of you rich. Now, a newbie will get stirred up and excited and link up with this character. In truth, they only see how your business can benefit their vision. They are asking you, in so many words, to help them to reach the peak of their successful mountains and in return, once they are there, they'll help you. You've got to know that you can't lift someone else up and think they'll come back down to lift you up. It is always a good idea to write and publish some rules to your business manual and site stating that you don't do these types of partnerships. Of course, you would word it more professionally, but you do need to beware of such characters. I've come in contact with many of these characters who swore that if I gave them a free service, or if I invested in their ideas, they would in return bless me when they got blessed. I've even had a few talk on and on about how confident they are in their business's or idea's success potential. Some of them are very convincing (the prefix of convincing is con...just so you'll know). This is what I call back alley partnerships. If they've got that much faith in their idea and they can convince you to come aboard, it's because you don't have that much faith in your idea. It is always good to interrupt them, since these characters will usually talk for over an hour trying to sell their ideas to you. You should politely interrupt them and refer them to your rules or read the rules to them. They may tell you that you are passing up on a million dollar idea, and they may tell you not to be like others who passed up on a great idea, but you have to remember that GOD gave you a baby to raise. You can't go over there, feed their baby (visions), and starve your own. Stay glued to your vision in faith and refuse to come undone.

<u>Wicked Counsel</u>

There will come a time when someone approaches you to hand you a list of unsolicited advice. This person may truly believe that their advice is good and will help you, and there are the ones who will purposely give you bad advice in hopes of harming you or your business.

Here's the thing...bad advice doesn't always look like bad advice. Many times, bad advice actually sounds pretty good. When placed next to wise counsel, sometimes bad advice will arouse your senses, whereas the good advice may not look so appealing. That's because our senses are temporal and are stimulated by anything that appeals to its lusts. Wise counsel, on the other hand, doesn't always appeal to our lusts, because wise counsel advises that we be patient, don't chase the money, let GOD lead, help others, and so on. Wise counsel comes against selfishness, whereas wicked counsel often appeals to our desires to be rich and lazy.

The counsel of a person is either good food for the soul, or it is poisonous to you and your destiny. Sadly enough, many people consume poisonous words because the people serving them appear to be friends or people looking out for their best interest.

Even "educated" advice isn't always good. As I mentioned earlier, I have never went to school for what I'm doing. I didn't go to college; therefore, I wasn't educated by man's system when it came to producing, strategizing, or marketing. I learned from GOD through trial and error. The LORD would often speak to me before I made a mistake, but I went forward anyway because I wanted to see what would happen. I learned to trust the voice coming from within, because I realized that it was HIS voice. As time went on, I came across many souls who were educated by the world's system, and their businesses weren't doing so well. As a matter of fact, the majority of them had to go back to work in secular America, and they wanted to know what kept me afloat. For me, it's not what kept me afloat; it's who kept me afloat. GOD kept me afloat, and I could never take that away from HIM. I had to listen to HIM (don't fake it), believe what HE was telling me (faith it), and apply it to my business (work it). There were times when HE told me to go against the grain of my understanding. For example, when the LORD told me to go up on my prices, I was hesitant because I thought that I would lose customers. I finally surrendered, and my business started getting more than twice as many customers as I'd previously gotten. Nevertheless, there were the ones who advised me against this because they were going with their understanding, whereas I was told to go against my own.

In mentoring others, I have found that the majority of new business owners are swamped with bad advice from other business and non-business owners. Please understand this: every business owner isn't a successful business owner, and every business owner does not want to see you successful in your business. Many people go by the law of seniority, and they believe that because you are new, you should never arrive at success before they arrive there. So they will advise you only to keep you in the place they feel you should be in, and that's right behind them.

When some of the girls that I'd mentored launched out and did opposite of what their original "advisers" had instructed them, they were met by some of the harshest words, followed by that person disassociating themselves from them. These self-erected advisers were never solicited by these women; they just came forward and started trying to insert themselves into their businesses. That's because they saw the potential in the business to succeed, and they saw the potential in the business owner to be successful. So they tried to insert themselves to cause the fall of that person's business or to put their hands in the piggy bank of that business. If someone truly wanted to see you succeed, they would NEVER get angry at you for not taking their advice.

A little hint of bad counsel could take down a large corporation. That's why many of the largest companies today have shareholders and several people that are decision makers running the company. They have to come together and come up with an agreement. This is to keep one man from having absolute power over that business. One man with too much power may get infected with pride, swell up with selfishness, and explode with bad ideas. Now, if a little bad advice could take down a large corporation, imagine what it could do to your company. You have to shut off all the noise to hear GOD. Even the advice that sounds good can be great-tasting poison that tingles as it goes down but destroys once it has settled in. All Satan needs to do is sow one bad seed into your business and watch it patiently grow over the years, until it is big enough to consume your business.

Every person that gives you advice doesn't have your best interest in mind. The best thing to do with advice is not to apply it, but to compare it to what GOD is saying to you. If it doesn't match up with what HE told you; it came from the devil. If you haven't heard from GOD, simply take the advice before HIM and pray about it, and don't move on it until you've heard back from HIM. Ask HIM to sift the advice and whatever is not good, let it fall beneath your feet. If someone is rushing you to do something, but you haven't heard back from GOD yet, don't do it. The enemy will rush you towards a decision to keep you from hearing GOD and applying what GOD said. He knows that the answer is given the minute you ask the question, but you have to be still and be obedient to hear it. Therefore, Satan will stir you up and tell you that the opportunity is a once in a lifetime opportunity, and that you are crazy for not taking it in haste.

Don't look at how many years a person has been in business because, again, some people operate with that seniority complex. To them, you don't have the right to access success until you've walked in failure the same amount of time that they've walked in failure. In addition, don't just take advice just because it tickles the ears and sounds good as it makes its way from your ears to your mind. Remember...antifreeze tastes good, but does that mean that we should drink it?

Keep your focus on helping people and being the best at what you do, and success will come if you don't invite failure in. I don't care how long someone has gone to school; they don't always have the right advice for YOUR business. The schools take their knowledge from textbooks and studies, but many of those studies were not conducted outside of middle-class America. In addition, if you are a minority, you must know that many of those studies were not conducted using minorities. So if your market is, for example, African American men around the ages of 25 to 35, it wouldn't be a good idea for you to apply that advice. That's like trying to catch water with a doughnut. What you have to do yourself is test the market and understand that the first year in business isn't always the most lucrative as far as money goes, but it will provide you a wealth of knowledge and understanding. This knowledge and understanding will help to sustain your company's success as you go along. In other words, you'll know better.

Federal and State Law Reminders

Please note that each law differs state to state unless it is a federal law. Check with your city clerk or state representative for more accurate information as to the laws that affect you.

1. (Federal Law) Each new business is required to apply for a TIN (Taxpayer Identification Number.) In some cases, you will be able to use your Social Security Number, but it is always best to get a TIN to avoid conflicts with the IRS.

2. (Federal Law) Any and every business in the United States that earns $400 or more in a calendar year is required to file taxes whether it is online or a brick and mortar store.

3. (State) Many states, if not all of them, can only tax you on the goods and services that you provided to another customer in that state. What this means is if you live, for example, in the state of Arkansas and your customer is in Arkansas, then you are required to pay taxes on that transaction, but if your customer is from New York, you may not be required to pay

taxes on that transaction. Check with your state tax office for more information.

4. (Federal) If you are an employer, you are required by federal law to withhold income tax, social security tax, and medicare tax from every employee every pay period.

5. (Federal) An EIN (Employer Identification Number) is required for any and every business that intends to hire employees.

6. (Federal) When you label someone an employee, you fall under the federal and state label of an employer. As such, you are required to pay the employee a minimum wage as set by federal law. In addition, in some states, if you don't schedule the employee a certain amount of hours each week, that employee can file for unemployment for the weeks that they do not acquire these hours. As an employer, you may be required to pay the employee benefits such as, but not limited to: health insurance, unemployment, vacation, and retirement. The Small Business Administration has broken down the differences in more detail here: http://www.sba.gov/content/hire-contractor-or-employee.

7. (Federal) An independent contractor is not the same as an employee. An independent contractor has their own business, must file for their own TIN Number, pays taxes on their own business, and renders services to you that are paid only upon completion of that service. The Small Business Administration has broken down the differences in more detail here: http://www.sba.gov/content/hire-contractor-or-employee.

8. (State and Federal) Oral contracts can be legally binding, but the problem is, it's hard to prove that the contract even exists. Nevertheless, hiring an attorney to defend yourself, plus taking time off from working to build your case, can be time consuming. Verbal agreements can get lost in words. Your client may honestly misunderstand you, or you may agree to

something and not remember the terms of it. This is why it is always better to put it in writing.

Knowing the laws that can and may affect your business can be the difference between staying in business and being sued out of business. Having a Christian business or being a Christian won't exempt you from the laws, nor will it cause others to refrain from trying to misuse your services. Study the laws of your state and know your rights and the rights of your clients before you start a business.

Recognizing Your Market

Not knowing who your target market is will always prove to be fatal to the life of your business. Sadly enough, this is a common stumbling block, especially with first-time business owners. Imagine someone opening a toy store in a senior living community. Sure, they'd get a few sales from doting grandparents, but they would more than likely not get enough sales to keep them in business. Where would you open up a toy store if this was your marketing arena? Think about it for a few seconds. Now, someone that does not understand marketing would just go and rent an affordable building, place a huge plush toy outside, and watch the traffic zoom on by. To sell toys, you can't just think like a child, but you have to think like a parent. Would you go out of your way to stop at a toy store? Not likely, unless it was the Christmas holidays or one of your children's birthday. This is why the most common place to find a toy store is in a mall or a shopping center. The parents have already stopped to get the things that they want and need, and oftentimes, they'll go ahead and give in to their children's pleas to enter the toy store. It's not out of the way, and this is convenient shopping.

When launching your business, you have to think along those lines. If you are setting up a physical location, it is always good to see how the surrounding markets will affect your business. It is also good to see how your neighborhood will affect your business. Apartment communities and homes near shopping centers usually cost more than other living communities that are further away because this is a convenience to the people living in those communities. It is also a convenience for the shop because they will have a loyal base of customers.

How does one recognize their market? You do this through research, and some are just common sense. One of my services that I offer is web design. Web design is a broad marketing area because most businesses need and want websites. That sounds simple enough, right? Well, it isn't. There are different kinds of web designers; not to mention, as a designer, there are several areas that I won't touch. There are web developers and coders, simple web designers, flash designers, and so on. Each category of business also has a specific type of design that is common for that area; for example, my corporate customers prefer more still, corporate-type websites. My ministry customers love flash and an entertainment-type feel. The list goes on and on. My specialty is ministry design; therefore, I am a professional at putting together flashy-type websites. Corporate sites are good, and I'm pretty good at those as well, but flash is my baby. Therefore, my marketing arena is ministries and ministers. Ministers are usually 25 years old and up, with the majority of them being mid to late 30s all the way up to mid to late 60s. Most ministers aren't loyal customers because they rarely update their websites. In most instances, when updates are needed, rather than pay the previous designer, most venture off to find new designers. It's not anything personal against you; the issue that I have found is that many ministries are always looking to save a few bucks, and they want something absolutely new. So, designers that target ministries don't usually look for return visits and orders from current customers. Therefore, if you are trying to get into the design arena and you want loyal customers, you may want to go towards the corporate customers, since they are more loyal. The reason is they charge their clients per service; therefore, they can empathize with you, but a lot of ministries simply believe that they shouldn't have to pay for updates. (Now, this is just ministries when they deal with a small business or with a business owner that they can see, but I believe it may be different when dealing with companies on a larger scale.) You have to know your clients' behaviors by studying their behaviors. Now, when someone is paying a monthly update cost, however, they are likely to stay with their current designer.

We are living in the age of technology, so it's pretty easy to find and locate your market simply through Internet research. You can also test the market and note the age range, gender, ethnicity, and social income status of all of your customers. This will help you to draw a conclusion and know where to setup your business. You may conclude, for example, that 80% of your customers are white females, mid to late 30s, in average income homes. This information is fundamental to your business's pulse. Therefore, you would know not to set up shop in a Latino community. As I stated before, most businesses do this and end up going out of business because they thought people were going to drive across state lines to get to them, when people look for two things when shopping: price and convenience. You can have the right price, but you're too far away and end up losing your customers to your high-priced competitor who happens to be conveniently located.

But what if you are running an online business? How do you market to your target audience? By promoting and selling on sites where your target market frequents. Let's take Facebook, for example. You can set your Facebook where your friends are your target market arena by sending out friend requests to the people who meet your market's description. If I wanted to sell briefcases, my target market would be professional males, aged 23-60. I would send out friend requests to professional men who met my marketing description.

Again, one of the best ways to test and recognize your target market is by giving away discounted services. This is also a great way to establish your portfolio. Don't discount your products or services too severely; otherwise, people who wouldn't ordinarily purchase them will get them just because the prices are reasonable.

Identify your demographic.
- What is the race of the majority of your clients?
- What is the gender of the majority of your clients?
- What is the age group of the majority of your clients?
- What is the marital status of the majority of your clients?
- What income range is the majority of your clients?
- What is the level of education of the majority of your clients?
- What is the profession of the majority of your clients?
- What is the location of the majority of your clients?

After you have identified the demographics that are more likely to buy your products and services, it is good to conduct marketing research by testing each demographic through target marketing. For example, let's say that you were selling caffeine cookies. These new cookies that you came up with are great for replacing that morning cup of coffee, plus they're filling. You tested the gender market and found that most of your customers were men. The next study would be to determine what race, income status, level of education, and profession are the men that are most likely to buy your cookies. You could give out free cookies to one hundred people who have agreed to visit the link on your business card and fill out the survey. Your survey would consist of the necessary questions to help you determine where and how to market your products.

Online product and service marketing is the craze of today, since it doesn't require trying to stop people as they hurry on to their next destination. You could allow people to purchase your products or services at discounted rates, or you can give them the service or product freely and ask them to fill out the online survey afterward. In addition, there are many online and offline research companies that you can hire to perform the necessary research for you.

The No-No Of Underpaying Yourself

I know that you want to offer low and competitive prices. So you set your prices extremely low and find yourself getting customers of the worst caliber. People who underpay themselves usually close their businesses within the first year and go back to work in the secular market. This is because they weren't earning enough, but they were working too much.

You're going to get two kinds of customers; one that pays you what you require with no questions, and one that wants to pay you as little as possible. The customers who'll pay you what you ask without complaint are usually the ones that will be there working exclusively with you for years and years to come. They usually don't overwork you either because they have come to know and recognize the quality in your work. If you can garner enough customers like this, you'd be able to successfully run your business without fail for a lifetime. I have customers like this, and they are never a problem to work with. In fact, they'll simply place an order with me and just say, "Do what you think is best; I trust you." The customers who are always trying to talk you down aren't loyal customers. They have a wrongful relationship with money, and because of this, they've submitted themselves to keeping it at all costs. So, they'll try to talk you down on your price and then try to get you to add extras to their product buys or services. As soon as someone comes along who offers cheaper products and services than you, they will go to them. For me, I come across both kinds of customers, but the smooth-talking or fast-talking ones, I happily release back to the wild. They will close your business down if you let them because, again, they love and trust their money and don't want to part ways with it.

When you underpay yourself, what's going to happen is you'll eventually lose interest in your business and become bitter. Not to mention, you'll get a lot of "cheap" customers, and these are the ones that are looking to get the most for the least. Your goal should be to get and maintain a loyal customer base who pays. In return, you should always give them the best products and services on the market. Don't mistreat the cheap ones, but you need to know when someone is not worth putting up with. Some may be tolerable because they'll learn your rules and learn that they can't get around them, but many are manipulative and argumentative, and these are the ones that you may have to send away. If you are looking to launch a business that spans across your state's lines and eventually grows to epic proportions, then you will have to learn to manage your business in a firm and professional way.

It is always good to offer lower prices than others, if you can, but only if this doesn't affect your life or lifestyle. As a professional, you should earn more money working for yourself than you did working for someone else. Too many business owners settle for the same wages that they were earning in the secular workplace, and this almost always backfires. It backfires because, in business, you will find some months are great and some are not so great. In those not so great months, they are actually making less than what they did in the outside work market, and consequentially, many fall behind on their bills and start filling out job applications.

Then, there are the ones that are afraid of a million dollar business. I have heard so many people say that they just want enough to live on and that's it. When I inquired as to their reasoning for settling, I have found that many believe that to want millions is sin. They don't usually come outright and say this, but they do say things like, "I don't want to be greedy. I just want enough to take care of my children and myself." When questioned further, it is easy to see that they've been taught to fear becoming a millionaire. People fear what's on the other side of a million. Many don't realize this until their business starts to grow and fear steps out of its high chair. They fear losing their families, being robbed, being used, or having to separate from what they know. Many who fear million dollar businesses actually speak against those that don't fear running such establishments. Personally, I'm not afraid of a million dollar or multi-million dollar business, but I don't lust after it, nor do I see riches as a chance to relax on a beach in Tahiti. I see millions as an opportunity to bless others who were like myself. GOD needs trusted souls to carry out HIS will on earth, and some of the things that are to be carried out require money. Unfortunately, many of the ones that HE allows to reach the million dollar mark simply don't give back enough.

Don't be afraid to be blessed, don't apologize for being blessed, and don't try to downplay your success trying not to offend others. Your success is come to glorify GOD and to establish HIS Kingdom here on earth.

When I was underpaying myself, I found that my attitude was less than friendly. I would be polite to my customer, but I would be frustrated with the work. "She wants me to do a web site *and* a logo for $199? And then she has the nerves to ask for a revision for the logo *and* a do over for the website?!" My frustration could be heard through the phone line. How dare someone try to take advantage of me, and here this person is allegedly Christian. That was until I discovered that my customers weren't the problem; I was. I was the one underpaying myself by posting up and accepting swap-meet prices for quality work. When I started charging my customers at a rate that I felt comfortable at and the rates that GOD gave me, the frustration began to subside, the work began to improve, and I got better customers.

What you will discover is that when you are asking for a reasonable rate, you'll get reasonable customers. Go down below what's reasonable, and you'll get customers who ordinarily can't afford your services, and they have a different way of thinking. They want it all! Everything that you can give them plus more. Have you ever seen a clothing store have a clearance sale where they'd marked their clearance down to $1? Now, this could be a store that ordinarily is considered expensive, and you'll find that store has its fair share of customers daily, but it's never packed. Nevertheless, they do pretty well on annual sales. Nevertheless, they are having a $1 sale, and the place is swarming with people that are trying to get their hands on those clearance racks. Many of them will knock you past security if you reach over them. After the sale, the store is torn up beyond recognition. This is to say that people have different classes of thinking. It's not so much class in relation to income, because you'll find that some of your customers may be below the poverty line and still pay you without fail. That's because their mind is not below the poverty line. Give them a little time, and they'll come out of poverty in body because their mind isn't there. Then, you may come across the well-to-do clients who aren't living in poverty, but their minds are there. They will try to get as much as they can for as little as they can. They'll be argumentative and manipulative because their love of money has made them self-centered. They are spiraling towards poverty in body because their minds are there. Like that store, they will tear your business to pieces if you let them. It is always good to identify the class of mind that your customer has rather than categorizing your clients by social economic status. Running your own business will teach you a lot about mindsets and strongholds, but the key is not letting that stronghold get a hold on you.

When you underpay yourself, you are basically trading your services and your products for someone else's lack. Research the going rates and test the market by offering a sale, for example, for the first seven customers. You need to see how much you have to pay out and how much you'll actually net and then measure it up by the time you spent performing the service or preparing the product. If it's not worth it, you're underpaying yourself and undercharging your customers.

The No-No Of Overcharging Your Customers

Greed. What an ugly word and an ugly reality. Go into the stores or businesses of some people, and you'll walk out of there just as fast as you went in because they are overcharging their customers. Sometimes it's greed, and other times it's lack of marketing knowledge, lack of funds, or an abundance of bad advice.

We won't assume, however, that you would overcharge your customers due to greed, but people do this all the time. I see Christian businesses launching all the time with ridiculously priced products and services and then, after a year or so, the business is closed. It's hard enough trying to run a Christian business without adding overpricing to it. When speaking with some of the owners, they happily proclaim that they will be rich within a year. A few months later, they are mad at the world and their church for not buying their ebook for $39.99 or for not buying their homemade pound cakes for $49.99.

When selling products, one of the most common reasons for

overcharging is when the buyer (owner) only buys the minimum amount of products. Companies usually sell their products in bulk; the more you buy, the more you save. When you buy the least amount of products, you'll pay the highest amount per unit. Then, there are shipping costs added to your initial costs. Of course, you want to get your money back, so your ankle bracelets may be selling at $19.99, while someone else is selling that same bracelet for $12.99. It is always better to buy as many of that product as you can so that you can offer reasonable rates to your customers. When you try to hold onto a few bucks, you're actually asking your customer to take the fall for you. We live in an age where that customer can easily research your product and find it at a more reasonable rate. I do this. If I go into a store and I like, for example, a shirt, but they are being unreasonable with their prices; I look at the tag and memorize the name of the company. I then conduct my own search for that shirt, and I'm usually able to find it at a more reasonable rate. Now, I do believe in paying a person what they ask, but if that person is just being ridiculous with their mark-ups, it's okay to walk away.

Sometimes, people overcharge because of their lack of funds. Yes, this is unfortunate, and my heart goes out to the business owner who is simply trying to make it with what he or she has. My advice is to always seek out markets that you can afford to stay afloat in. In truth, there are some markets that you don't have to have a lot of money to jump into. You simply need to know how and where to market your business. In addition, it is always good to seek out professional help so that you can get the knowledge that you need to make it in today's market. Think of it this way: You can spend thousands trying new and failed products, or you can spend under a thousand to hire a professional that will teach you what you need to know. Oftentimes, someone on the outside can show you what you're doing wrong on the inside.

Then, there's the bad advice crew. Yes, they are out there, and they've got dreams for you because their dreams for themselves are having nightmares. They haven't researched anything, but they believe that you should be able to earn $199 per baseball cap that you sell because the cap will have the customer's picture on it. As if someone can't look down and see their faces already. So they excitedly pep you up, wind you up, and send you out as today's entertainment. Twelve laughs later and a buck short, you look for them and they are nowhere to be found. They are out giving away their counsel to the next young dreamer without a clue.

Business is just like marriage. You can easily get advice from others, but it is always better to get advice from someone who's had not just a business, but have run and continue to run a successful business. Your customers are coming for quality services, quality products, and affordable pricing. Don't sacrifice one for the other. Look out for your customers and many of them, in return, will look out for you.

Finally, there is lack of marketing knowledge. This simply means that the business owner just didn't know any better. Having a business without having the necessary knowledge is like having a store open with empty shelves. Knowledge is as crucial to your business as the products and services themselves. A lot of times, people complain about not liking to read, but if it's necessary, you have to put your personal likes and dislikes behind you so that you can launch your business properly. Most first-time business owners believe that launching a business is simply telling people that they provide a service and then waiting for business. Needless to say, it's not like that. You have to be knowledgeable about the products and services that you sell, and you need some marketing knowledge. You need to know how and where to market your business. You need to know what works and what does not work. Ask the average first time business owner who their target market is, and they'll proudly say that anyone in the world can order from them. People think that by broadening their hopes for who will order will increase their sales, but it's quite the opposite. You have to actually market that product or service, and if you don't have billions of dollars, you won't be able to market it to the whole wide world. In addition, why spend millions marketing Christian t-shirts to a Muslim country? You need to know your market, and you need to know the shopping behaviors of your target market. For example, pantyhose sales are at their peaks on Saturdays and Sundays. This is because women are ordinarily preparing to go to church on Sunday morning. This is why many major markets try to ensure that their pantyhose racks are fully stocked before the onset of the weekend. There are also certain holidays that mark the peak of pantyhose sales. You have to know your market's behavior so that you can behave accordingly.

You also need to know how to market. If you don't know, it is always good to tap into the free knowledge on the Internet. You can market through flyers, t-shirts, commercials, online advertisements, squeeze pages, and so on. In addition, one of the biggest offenses to your business is poor branding. It is always better to have no branding than it is to have low-budget looking branding.

Don't see your customers as your token to Beverly Hills because they won't appreciate being bled out like that. Instead, when your customer feels like you are looking out for their best interest (because you are), they'll become loyal customers.

<u>Preventative Maintenance</u>

There is maintenance, which simply means to maintain, and then there is preventative maintenance, which means to maintain by preventing something from occurring. Every business needs maintenance and preventative maintenance, but a lot of people don't play defense in their businesses.

Your business's preventative maintenance is your business rules, guidelines, contracts, attorneys, frequently asked questions, and so on. Let's face the truth: everyone that wants to do business with you won't be saved. It doesn't matter whether they sitting in a church, standing behind the pulpit in a church, or if they aren't in church at all. You will come across some characters that are fit for drama when you go into business for yourself. One of the funniest testimonies that I get from Christians that do business with Christians is how they started out thinking that everything was going to run smoothly. They were dealing with their brethren, so they were sure they didn't need rules, guidelines, contracts, and so on. Many of them testify that they would enter into verbal contracts because, again, their customer was Christian or allegedly Christian. Then came that first challenging customer who didn't want to operate by the rules, who was very condescending towards them, and who threatened to take them to court. They finally got rid of that customer and continued on doing business as they were doing in the beginning because they thought this was a one-time thing. Then, a few months later, another rude or manipulative customer comes on the scene and gives them more havoc than the first. At some point, the light comes on and they know that they simply cannot get around the rules, guidelines, contracts, and attorneys.

Rules and Guidelines: Your rules are set to protect you, protect your customer, and make the transaction a smooth one. Any business without rules is one where chaos will frequent. Sure, you may be a nice person, and you don't want to offend your customers by making them follow rules and guidelines. Rules might offend them, right? You are right! Rules are laws that offend common law-breakers, but people who are serious about doing business with you won't be offended by the presence of rules. In addition, you have to not only establish the rules, but enforce them. If you have rules that your customers learn that they can get around, your rules are for nothing. Word will get out that your business isn't guided by rules, and you'll get all kinds of shady customers as a result. Set rules, and you be the first one to honor those rules. Don't let your emotions or your customer's emotions cause you to overlook the rules. The same way people respect big companies is the same way they should respect yours.

F.A.Q.S (Frequently Asked Questions): Frequently asked questions are a great way to cut your phone calls in half by 25-50%. Pay attention to the questions that your customers frequently ask you. Jot down the questions and your answers to those questions. Publish them for your customers to see so that they won't have to call you for every little question that they have. Instead, they can always refer back to the FAQs on your website or flyer. You can also write questions and answers that you expect others to ask. Being proactive is better than being active.

Contracts: Rules, guidelines, and FAQs are great; but did you know that some of your customers will say that they never read them? In addition, they won't want to honor the rules because they won't feel like they should have to honor them because they didn't read them. Contracts are rule sheets that detail the rules, services, expectations, and requirements of both parties (owner and client.) Each contract requires a legally binding signature and can be used in a court of law. You're probably like tens of thousands of Christian businesses who have vowed not to ever sue their customers, but this doesn't mean that they won't try to sue you. A contract isn't just something you should get in the near future, but a contract is something you should have before you open your business's doors for the first time. You need to be protected from the minute you call yourself a business owner.

Attorneys: You can go around this option in the beginning. You can hire an attorney to create your contract, or you can hire another professional to create it. You can also create it yourself, if you know how to. The contract alone will act as your legal representative or your customer's legal representative. If you can't afford to retain a lawyer, the best thing to do is shop around for one and have him or her on standby. This way, should one of your clients decide to sue you, you'll already have someone that you can turn to for legal advice.

Employee Handbooks: Employee handbooks are essential if you have or plan to be hiring employees for your business. This handbook lays everything out for them to know, including what is expected of them, what can get them terminated, discipline procedures, expected pay and raises, employee insurance information, vacation pay, the amount of vacation hours allowed to full time and part time employees, and so on. Like a contract, this book is necessary if you intend to hire employees. Anyone can say that you made a verbal agreement with them, but what is written will prove or disprove their claims.

Independent Contractor Handbooks: Independent contractors are not the same as employees; therefore, they need a handbook all their own. In this guide, you will mention the fact that they are an independent contractor, they are not a part of your business (since independent contractors own their own businesses), what is expected of them, and so on. For example, independent contractors are required by law to fill out a W-9 form. Ordinarily, the employer is to retrieve this information from the c and submit it to the IRS.

Also, check your state and federal listings to see what is expected of local businesses. It is better to be safe than sorry.

Your Web Presence

Whether you are or are not running an online company, you need a web presence. A local presence only makes you available to local buyers, but a web presence makes you available to people around the world. Even if you own a company that only deals locally, a web presence will serve as an open door to your immobile customers as well. Someone may want to hire you to do a job, but they may not have a car, their car may be in the shop, or they may have a physical handicap that prevents them from coming into the store. In addition, your web presence will help your customers to competitively shop between you and your competitors. Some people may even travel that extra distance when they see that you are offering the same services at better rates than your competition. A web presence is like your building, only online. It is a store that people can come in 24 hours a day and look around.

As I stated earlier, it is better to do no branding than it is to brand your business in an unappealing way. Your customers will believe whatever your branding says over whatever your ads are saying. So if your ad reads, for example, that you are the number one dealer of hub caps in the city, but your branding looks like you're dealing hub caps in a dark alley, your customers will see you as a low budget company that one should enter only when in desperation. Therefore, they'll head up to another hub cap shop just because their website and their branding made them look like a super dealer. Once they get to the place, however, they may find that the building looks nothing like the ads, but it still gives the owner or the customer service reps the opportunity to show them what they have available and possibly sell them. When ordering your website, please look for professional designers that can make your business look like a multimillion dollar establishment. Don't opt out the cheap way trying to save a few hundred or a few thousand bucks. Sometimes, you can get the work done for a fraction of the cost, only you need to shop around and be sure to look at the designers' portfolios. Google their names and their business names and type the word "review" behind their names to see what their customers are saying.

Then there is your domain name. Your domain name should be your company's name and not your own personal name unless you are doing business under your own personal name. If my name was Sally Doe and I was selling shoes, I wouldn't buy www.sallydoe.com because people will associate the name with a person. Now, over time, if you're doing business under your name and the word gets out about your company, you may be able to operate under your name. The company Tiffany's was able to keep up with demand and become innovators in jewelry making. So, if you want to use your name, go right ahead, but you need to have enough money to advertise your company so that people will know what you are doing and selling. You can also choose to purchase multiple domain names and point them to one name. Let's say that your company's name is Sally Doe and you sell pet supplies. Since the name Sally Doe has nothing to do with pet supplies, you can choose a domain name that markets your service and still have www.sallydoe.com. For me, I would go with something like www.petsuppliesbysally.com. Once the visitor clicks on the website, they would find themselves on www.sallydoe.com. This is called domain forwarding, and it's pretty easy to do. Your domain provider could help you with this setup, and it usually takes about 5 minutes and under to point a domain name. Now, the name that is the forwarding domain name will not show up in Google searches; therefore, we want to choose the domain name that is more likely to generate traffic as your main domain and the other one as your forwarding domain. If you want both names to show up in Google, you'll need two websites. You can have one set up as an intro page and once they click it, they are automatically forwarded to your main site. This would allow for both domains to show up in Google. For example, my seal and logo site is called "Anointed Fire Seal and Logo Translations" and my domain name is www.afsalt.com. But generating traffic to that domain is no easy task unless I am specifically advertising that domain name and sending traffic to it, or unless someone else is specifically advertising that domain name and sending traffic to it. The site gets quite a few visitors each day from me advertising it, but there are people who are looking for seal and logo designers on Google. How did I bring them my way? I used a common term and purchased the domain name www.thesealofthebishop.com. This gave me a top Google ranking, and it generated traffic that hadn't seen my ads to the site. I pointed the domain name to a second site, and I use that site as an intro page to my main site.

You may be saying that having two sites is costly, but it's quite the contrary. You just have to have the patience to shop around.

When choosing a domain name, you should always choose one that is short and to the point. If your business's name was Sally Does Desktop Computers and Software, it wouldn't be a good idea to purchase www.sallydoescomputersandsoftware.com. People actually do this and this hurts their search engine listings; not to mention, people won't remember all of those letters. Nobody wants to go through typing long domains, knowing that they will more than likely mess up and be on a not found page. Instead, the wise thing to do here is to see if www.sallydoes.com is available and buy a second domain called www.sdcomputers.com. What Sally Doe is doing is making it easier for her customers to find her. Sure, the ones that know her company personally can easily Google her name and find her site. Then, they can click that long link and start their shopping, but would you want to limit yourself only to your current customers, or are you looking to add more customers?

Whatever domain name you choose, you ought to use that same extension as much as possible. So, if you open up a Facebook fan page, you should choose sdcomputers as your URL for Facebook, Twitter, Linkedin, and other popular sites. You can also start these pages with the headers, "Computers and Software by Sally Doe," rather than "Sally Does Computers and Software." You're not changing the name, and they will see your actual business name when they come into your business and when they visit your website. The goal here is to generate traffic and establish your online presence. Believe it or not, whenever you use an extension and you don't use that extension everywhere online, someone else will take advantage of that and use it for their own company. Their goal is to generate your traffic to their website.

When purchasing a domain name, it is always good to get the four major domain extensions (.com, .net, .org and .info.) Godaddy will usually give you a pretty decent deal on bulk buys. This way, you don't just buy .com and someone else taps into your traffic by buying .net or .org. People do this! I hear it all the time where some disgruntled business owner has discovered that another company is capitalizing on their cheapness. Let's call it what it is. They didn't buy the domains because they were looking at the dollar signs and didn't want to spend that extra few bucks. Somebody else conducted a search and saw that they had a pretty decent looking company that appears to be a traffic generator. Their company was selling the same thing, so they decided to tap into the traffic.

Are they thieves? Depends on how you look at them. Some people would call them innovators, smart, or determined; while others would call them thieves. They can't actually use your name if it's registered, but they can sit close to your domain name with their own. To stop someone from buying an afsalt domain, I bought them all. To stop someone from buying an anointedfire domain, I bought them all (www.anointedfire.com, www.anointedfire.org, www.anointedfire.net, and www.anointedfire.info). If your name should ever rise to the major leagues, people will begin looking for variations of your name to register to tap into your traffic. That's why you have to think proactively and purchase them while you're still playing in the little leagues.

I often come in contact with quite a few "budgeted" people who refuse to spend those extra few dollars and get those domain extensions. They often tell me that they don't have a lot of money to spend, and this is why they didn't buy the domain extensions. Then, while they are explaining to me why they didn't do it, I have had one or two to put me on hold and place an order: "Give me a number one, large with a coke. Oh yeah, add an apple pie on the side." Yes, they have to eat, but ask some of today's biggest names in business about the sacrifices that they had to make. Some of them would go home and eat a peanut butter sandwich or cook something that was in the fridge (if they had a home) and use that $8.88 to buy a domain name or whatever they needed. Being on a budget is not the same thing as being cheap. To get different results, you must be prepared to live a different lifestyle than what you're accustomed to. The problem with many business owners isn't that they don't have the funds to purchase what they need (logos, websites, domains, flyers, etc.); the problem is they have a preference as to what they want to do with the extra money that they have left after bills. They don't want to sacrifice that desire to dine out today for an opportunity of a lifetime. I've seen ladies trying to spend their last getting hairpieces when their sites weren't even up. This is an error in thinking, because when you are serious about your business, it will show. Until then, nobody can help you out.

On the flip side though, I have met and mentored a few who were absolutely great to work with. They will take their last and invest it into their future. That's what sowing is. It's taking the seeds that you have to grow up the harvest that you want. It is always easy to spot someone headed towards success because of their way of thinking. Money has lost its powerful grip on them, and they have learned to stop chasing money. As a result, in a year or two, money is chasing them all over the place.

Take a moment out to Google your business name. What do the results look like? If you haven't launched out there yet, you won't see any listings of your business; maybe some that share the same name or some like yours. Your online presence needs to be a strong one. Coming up in one page of Google search results is not a good thing, because this shows that you don't do much business. Again, people believe what they find online about you. How can you increase your listings on Google and other major search engines? Place your website link up on every site you enter.

Here are some things that you can do to create a strong web presence:
1. Create profiles on every site that relates to what you are doing or is just a site where people come together. Use your business extension, if you can customize the URL.
2. Create a blog and blog about your business at least once a week.
3. Leave comments on other blogs, if the owner allows you to do so.
4. Create profiles on sites that localize listings such as www.manta.com.
5. Ask your current customers to leave a testimony about your business, either on your site, blog, or ask them to create a blog. You can also set up a Google Reviews account.
6. Create a signature in your email with your web links and

business motto in it.

7. Log in online and post up something once a week at least (once a day, if you can.)

8. Update your website often and keep it interactive.

Punctuality Counts

There are many aspects to being a great business owner, but it takes a few mistakes to be labeled a bad one.

Delivering the product or service in a timely manner is essential to keeping the doors of your business open. A lot of business owners do not realize the importance of being effective, efficient, and punctual.

I sometimes have to contract external businesses to do some work for me when my workload is heavy or when my schedule doesn't permit me to do the extra work. Many times, I like to send the work to new start-up businesses because I want to see them succeed. Whenever I see that the person moves by their feelings as opposed to going ahead and tackling the workload, I don't send them anymore of my customers because I believe that good customer service is wholly good. Punctuality is never to be sacrificed because of how you feel.

There are days when I wake up and I get orders that I would rather not have gotten, for example. I love designing logos, and websites are fun as well, but web content is not fun for me.

When I get orders for services that I provide but don't like to do, I usually have to force myself to sit down and do the work. I want to tackle other "fun" projects or start a new project of my own, but that order still looms over my head, and I can't rest until I tackle it. I had to learn not to work by feelings but to just do the work; after all, I am a business owner, and I can't let my emotions have a partnership in my business. When I work with people who do let their feelings have a key to their doors, I vow not to ever work with them again because their choices directly affect my business.

A great example was a customer that came along and wanted to order some web content from me. Again, I absolutely do not like to tackle web content and I had a workload, so I sent the order to another woman who was trying to launch her business. I put the customer in direct contact with her, and I trusted her to fill the order in a timely manner. The customer wanted to pay her a deposit, but I told her to require 100% upfront for writing assignments because there is no way to show the customer the work and protect the work from theft. Anyhow, after she got the order, I tried not to mention the work to her because I wanted her to do business the way she thought business ought to be done. If she wanted to keep me posted, that would have been great because that's what you do when someone sends an order to you, but if she didn't want to keep me posted, I knew not to send any more business to her.

Immediately after receiving payment, she said something that let me know that I was never to send any more work to her. She said to me that she didn't feel like starting the work, and that she was going to put it off for a few days. This is a no-no when owning a business because your customer is trusting you with their business, and you should want them to become repeat customers and refer more business to you. That's where a lot of your business is going to come from; word of mouth. I didn't say anything because, again, I believe in keeping my opinion to myself unless otherwise asked. A few weeks later, she said that the customer had been calling her about the project, and she'd basically been rude with him. He even threatened her by saying that he was going to call me, and she taunted him by telling him to call me, but he never did. She told me these things out of her own mouth, and I was beside myself, but I'm not an argumentative person, so I held my peace and let her be as open as she wanted to be. Needless to say, I never sent another customer her way and we went on with our separate lives.

You may be surprised at her gall, but she actually said what other business owners think; she just said it aloud. People often want the paycheck, but they don't want the work. Your human side will always kick in, and there will be days when you absolutely don't want to do any work, but you've got to be more dedicated to your own business than you were to your secular job. In the secular workplace, you have to come to work no matter how you feel. You honor what they require of you because you want that paycheck. When you are working in your own business, you have to be even more dedicated than that. The hardest part of it all is overcoming yourself, not your customer. You will get some good customers and you will get some not so great customers, but your goal should be to provide excellent customer service and products at affordable rates in a timely manner.

Here are a few tips to help you get over yourself when running a business:
1. Just do it! It doesn't matter if today is a holiday and people on secular jobs are off; you should never take a day to lounge around unless it is absolutely needed.
2. Get over yourself. The hardest part about business ownership is giving up those repetitive ritualistic acts that you've grown accustomed to and learning to adapt to a schedule.
3. Sometimes you need to just take 50% down when performing a service so that you'll stay motivated. A lot of times when people get the full payment in their hands, they begin to lose interest in doing the work

because it feels to them like they aren't being paid. They lose their zeal and oftentimes, once the zeal is gone, bad customer service comes in. To curb this, if you are performing a service, ask the customer for 50% payment upfront and request the other 50% once you've finished the work before you send the work to them. I had to do this at one point to fight my human side off as well until I learned to do better.

4. Don't take anyone's kindness for their weakness. We often say that to others in relation to ourselves, but this has to be a two-way road. You will often get customers that are super kind and at the same time, you will get some super rude customers. A lot of entrepreneurs give great customer service to their rude customers, trying to calm them down and satisfy them, but they mishandle their good customers. Rude people tend to do business with people whom they feel they can control with their attitudes, whereas a gentle spirit simply loves your work and will be the one to refer the most customers to you. Don't give kind Kelly's extra time to rude Roy just because he's cranky. Instead, treat all of your customers with kindness, and any time you get one that is over the top rude and hard to please, don't be afraid to send them away. People like that actually help close businesses.

5. Give yourself a schedule and abide by it no matter how you feel. Sometimes we get over on ourselves because we can, but we forget that there is a customer waiting for their service or product. Be at work on time every day, or fire yourself until you get a better attitude.

Distractions Versus Actions

If you've ever had your own business, you will know that business ownership comes with its fair share of distractions and challenges. The number one distraction always comes from within the business owner him or herself. The number two distraction is the cost of business ownership, setup, and maintenance. Other distractions include, but are not limited to personal relationships, legal matters, unruly customers, and so on. When you decide to become a business owner, you have to know everything that you are signing up for. Becoming a kingdom entrepreneur is not just going in and harvesting the perks of financial freedom, but it is also weathering the storms that precede financial freedom. These storms are often pretty rough, but they don't come to flood you out; they come to water you. It's how you view these storms that will determine whether or not you make it through and transition from a Christian business to a successful Christian business. Again, they are not one and the same.

Have you ever paid attention to ducks on a lake? Well, a mother duck will lead her baby ducks from one side of the lake to the other. She's teaching them to swim and hunt for themselves, but oftentimes, she loses more than 80% of her children on that lake as she leads them. There are many predators around that are looking for something to snack on, and a baby duck is high on a predator's wish list. Normally, the ones that stay closest to their mother are safe, but the ones that become distracted and wander away are usually taken or swallowed whole. The remaining ducklings learn to stay closer to mother, and they grow up to repeat the cycle.

GOD is leading you, and with your business, you have to stay close to HIM. There are many who have Christian businesses who are distracted by the things around them, and they always end up getting taken or swallowed whole. They are distracted by money, greed, people, doubt, fear, and so on. Because they have left the safety of FATHER'S wings, they find themselves becoming prey to every hungry devil around them. This is why it is absolutely imperative for you to stay close to the FATHER and go along with HIM even when you don't know where HE'S taking you.

One of the most common distractions is fear. People are afraid of success, and people are afraid of failure. So to avoid the two, they decide to keep living the way that they know how to live. This way, they feel that they haven't failed, and they can easily convince themselves that success is just not for them. This is that distraction from within that we label as a "self" distraction, where a person convinces themselves that they are not cut out for success or whatever follows success. Let's be truthful here; success brings about a whole new set of problems that an unsuccessful person has never had and will never have. It is normal to worry about these problems, but GOD prepares you along the way to success for what you will encounter. Many of what serves itself as a problem for other business owners won't come near you because wisdom will be guiding you. They may tell you that this issue will come upon you, but in truth, it only came upon them because they skipped the necessary seasons. You should simply cancel their words and keep going forward. Don't let their fear overpower you just because they are under its feet. This is why you should never try to speed towards success, but instead, you should always be willing to let the seasons play out so that the necessary rains can come and water you; the necessary storms can come and empower you, and the necessary fall-aways can occur to release you for elevation. You see, during this process, many people press the stop button because they don't like what's happening, but the process is necessary. It's like when you ask GOD to bless you and your wife with that big house on the hills. You believe GOD for it, and then some things begin to occur that you don't like. People often think that they are under attack when they are not. Instead, what is happening is the great falling away is taking place so that you and your wife can be elevated. GOD knows who is a danger to you, your family, and your business. GOD knows who would be a danger to you once you have reached a certain height in HIM. Some people can be great friends when you live in the same realm as them, but dare to elevate, and you'll need a spiritual restraining order. You may pray that the LORD blesses you with your own successful business and then, all of a sudden, your boss comes out of nowhere and fires you. This doesn't mean you are under attack; don't be distracted! This could mean you are being prepared for your next level in HIM. Rather than rebuking and going into warfare, sometimes you simply need to ask the LORD what is going on and say to HIM, "FATHER, your will be done."

The monetary distraction occurs in someone with low-budget thinking or someone who is guarded by fear. Many people don't spend money; their money spends them. Their money tells them what it will and will not do. Their money tells them what it can and cannot do. They launch businesses and plan to do more once they've entered a new income bracket. Problem is, this will never happen when money is in control. You see, there is an adage out that mirrors on the truth and that is, "You have to spend money to make money." It looks like the truth, but there is one word that throws it off and makes it a lie, and that word is "spend." Instead, it should read, "You have to invest money or sow money to reap money." No one plants an apple seed to get a banana tree. If they did, they would be considered a certified nutcase. The problem here is too many people are afraid of what's behind investing. Some people will run out there and pull on a slot machine (which is sin), but tell them to sow a seed and you'll get a blank stare. When a farmer sows seeds, he knows to expect a harvest. He waters the seeds and turns the ground to make sure that the seed gets the necessary sunlight, nutrients, and moisture. He also kills the weeds that threaten to grow up with his seed. A farmer doesn't just buy land, turn the dirt, and water the ground with no seeds in it. If he did, he'd get a harvest of happy weeds. A farmer must first buy seeds before he begins the sowing process. A farmer doesn't stop sowing seeds just because the crows keep stealing his crop. Instead, he buys or creates a scarecrow to scare them away. Some have even been known to dress as scarecrows, when the birds get too comfortable and scare them away so that they will continue to believe that the scarecrow is alive.

As a business owner, you are a farmer. You have seeds in your hands and yes, sometimes, you want to just consume them and be full. But a seed not sown is a dead seed. When you hear that familiar voice of your money or your fear trying to tell you where your money needs to go, remember that your money has been going there for years and it keeps giving you back the same reward. The best thing to do is to sow seeds where they count; in fertile ground! Seeds have one harvest when they are consumed, and that is when they are exposed from the bowels. If you don't believe that, go and buy yourself a lot of sunflower seeds and eat them. Then, wait for your harvest. Drink plenty of water and wait, because, just like seeds on the outside; seeds on the inside need water to complete the process.

One distraction that you are almost sure to get is from people who do not like or do not agree with what you're selling or how you're selling it. They'll come after you with words, lawsuits, and any other device that they can to bring you down. As a

Christian business, you'll find that most of the people that come against you are people claiming to be Christians. You shouldn't get this confused with actual men and women of GOD, but there are many impersonators that come on the scene. When I first started out, I advertised my seals and logos on Facebook. I don't think I tagged anyone, but on Facebook, your posts will show up in your friend's news feeds unless they have unsubscribed from your postings. Anyhow, I came to my computer one morning and logged into Facebook to the surprise of the day. Some woman had posted on my wall ridiculing me for posting up my designs in her feed. Again, I don't think I actually tagged her, but she simply saw the designs in her feed, and it must have been kryptonite for her. Anyhow, in her post, she attempted to bash me for posting up my designs, and then she suddenly went from flesh to claiming to be prophesying against me. I was surprised, but at the same time, I knew that GOD was NOT speaking through her. GOD is not flesh and is not stirred up just because we get irritated in the flesh by someone's action. Needless to say, I deleted her and moved on. A couple of months later, I get an inbox message from another woman. Taking one look at her, I could see witchcraft all over her before I even read the message. She tried to condemn me for designing seals and logos because, in her belief system, this was evil to do. Now, if I did not know the LORD, I would have done like many before me and retreated into the dark confines of their understanding. Instead, I stayed prayerful and even asked the LORD (the first time) if I was in error in any kind of way. HE confirmed that not only was I doing HIS will, but that I shouldn't be so quick to question HIS will. It is better and safer for me to question someone else's motives than HIS will.

If GOD is in your business, the devil will try to bring it down! He will impersonate GOD and try to find a way to discourage you. But if you have faith in GOD and you know HIS voice, you won't be moved by his antics. Don't complain just because somebody came up against your business. That's a blessing! Why would one even dare to think that Satan won't try to pull the plug on their business when it was established by GOD? That's like believing that Satan won't bother you after you've been baptized. You're going to come in contact with some that will look like a child of GOD, but they will tell you to do the opposite of what GOD told you to do. Don't you dare question GOD when you come in contact with this character. They are on demonic assignment, and you are being tested. Who do you believe? People love to play on a person's doubts if that person isn't grounded in the WORD. If you're a little shaky and always looking for a prophecy, you're the devil's favorite target because he knows that all he has to do is blow the winds of doctrine, false prophecies, and opinions your way; and you'll be on the other side of your emotions in little to no time. In your business, you have to take a firm and grounded stand in CHRIST. If you know GOD gave it to you, don't retreat for anyone. I don't care what color their cloak is, what their title is, or what they say to you. What GOD gives to you is your assignment. If I went to a school and gave a second grader a college student's assignment, chances are, he wouldn't be able to complete it. He's not at that level yet. Therefore, when someone says that they don't understand your assignment, it is clear that they are not at that level yet. Why put down your assignment and wait on them to level up? In order to do this, you have to literally step out of GOD'S will for your life and step into their will for your life.

Other people include family members and relationships that are not grounded in the LORD. Let's be truthful with ourselves here; a person after GOD'S own heart will always want you to pursue GOD'S will for your life. Someone that is not after HIS heart has another plan for you that is usually centered around themselves. This is why it is absolutely imperative to stay in the will of GOD in every aspect of your life and business. When you have one member in sin, it'll contaminate the whole body.

You will face many distractions, and it's easy to say that you'll face them like a lion robbed of her cubs, but when those challenges come face to face with you, your roar sounds more like a meow. This is to say that you need to prepare yourself to be the success story that GOD has called you to be, but be prepared for the distractions that come along the way. Sometimes, a distraction can't find you until you find yourself out of GOD'S will. Sometimes, a test will come along, but at that moment, you can present yourself as victorious or be presented as today's failure. Failure snacks on many Christian ministries each and every day, but victory lives in those that are built to last.

<u>Emotional Versus</u>
<u>Professional</u>

I had a customer who had placed an order for a logo. This was my first time working with her, and I am always happy to greet, meet, and work with new clients. Anyhow, my site has rules on it that guard the logo ordering process. These rules were put in place to protect myself, the customer, and to ensure that each transaction goes smoothly. One of the rules is the amount of revisions that are allowed per package. This customer got the least-expensive package, and I filled the order. The logo came out looking great, and everything was going well...or so I thought. I got a call back from the customer, and she wanted to make a change to the logo. The first change was an error of mine, which was a simple text correction, so of course, it was free of charge. The next day, she called and wanted to make another change, and since it was a simple change, I decided to charge her a lot lower than what was posted on my site for a revision. After all, the change was minor and the customer was new. I invoiced her; she made the payment, and I made the change for her. A day later, I get a call from her that she's changed her mind again and wants another change, but this time I tell her that I will have to charge her the regular fee. I could hear in her voice that she was not too happy with me, and she said that she'd just leave it as it was because she wasn't going to pay that kind of money for a change. After bidding her farewell, I hung up the phone knowing that this was probably not going to be one of my repeat customers, but here's the hard part: I had to learn to be okay with that.

As a Christian, my heart does go out to some of the customers, and I want to go outside of my rules to provide them with exceptional customer service. The human part of me feels an emotional pull when dealing with others, but GOD has told and taught me to remain firmly behind my rules as a professional. Why is that?

When you go outside of your rules, you are often led there by your emotions or the emotions of your client. Most of us don't like to hear a not-so-happy tone coming from the other end of the line or to see a not-so-pleased face standing before us; therefore, we often stretch our businesses out to accommodate emotions and emotional people. In business ownership, you absolutely cannot do this because you are teaching your customers how to deal with you in business, and they will run you out of business without giving it a second thought. You are like a glass sitting on the edge of a dresser. People look for a handle on you, and when they can't find it, they will unintentionally push you off and shatter you to pieces. Once your business has closed its doors, they'll happily find another business to rob with their emotions.

When you say to people that you are a Christian, one of the first things that they do in their minds is place you in a certain category, and they deal with you in the way that they deal with people in that category. Many people feel that they can stretch a Christian, but they would never do this to the world; even if they themselves are a Christian.

In talking to many business owners, I have found that they

often deal with this emotional pull that they put on themselves or that the customer puts on them. This is the time where they have to make a quick decision as to how they want to handle the situation. What keeps most business owners from giving in to the customer is the understanding of how a business is labeled amongst the people and how that label determines what types of clients that frequent the business. For example, if you had a store that let people get food on credit, you'd more than likely get a poor crowd, and the middle class to upper class patrons wouldn't do too much business with you. This is because of the label that you now have on your business. If you get a reputation for giving in to rude clients, you will find yourself dealing with a lot of rude clients because word is you will eventually back down.

Emotions close the doors to thousands of businesses every day. Additionally, I have heard many Christian business owners vow to never work with Christians again because of having dealt with so many emotional Christians, who didn't want to honor the rules or pay for the service or product they wanted. It's not the customer's fault; however, if you give in to their attitude trying to keep them as a customer. Many people who stretch you will eventually break you if you let them. There are many, many people who look for small businesses that are in a state of desperation so that they themselves can benefit from that business's desperation. It's like having a steak tied to a string and dangling it in front of a hungry man's face. People will dangle their cash and their business in front of you if you are desperate enough to chase it. They will make their demands and promise to give you what you are working to get if you do as they say. You can't do business like this! This type of mentality limits you to a small group of small-minded people that take advantage of anyone who lets them.

I had to get over how I felt to become a successful professional. I couldn't do business the way that people wanted me to do business because every man is often for himself. When I stopped doing what people demanded that I do, and I started doing what GOD told me to do, I began to lose the wrong kinds of customers and get the right kind of customers: people that pay well without question, complaint, or manipulation. This is the clientele that you need to succeed in your business. I had to get over how people felt and understand that the rules are the rules; even though I can change them, I won't, because that defeats the purpose of having them in the first place.

This is to warn you: don't let people run you out of business, and don't run yourself out of business with emotions, because emotions are rooted in flesh, and flesh roots itself in rebellion.

<u>Selling Yourself</u>

If you are running a business where you're required to be on the front-line and not behind the scenes, you will need to learn to sell yourself. Many of your customers will decide to work with you or not to work with you based on your presentation of yourself.

But how does one sell oneself, and what does it mean to sell one's self? Below is a list of suggestions that should help you:

1. Always know your crowd and market yourself accordingly. If I'm trying to sell motorcycles to a group of scarf-wearing, tattooed up men, it wouldn't be wise for me to come there wearing a scarf and tattoos. Many people would think otherwise, but the reason you shouldn't do that is because you are trying to deal with the individuals on a professional level and not a personal level. If you look like your customer to the point that they feel they can relate to you, they will try to deal with you in a like manner. Instead, I would come dressed professionally.
2. Always be polite, but firm. The misconception is that to

be firm, one has to be rude, and this is just not true. You have to be firm when it matters and polite always. For example, if a woman wanted to buy five pairs of shoes from your company, and she wanted a discount, you would firmly tell her that a discount is not available. At the same time, you'd be polite about it. In many of these cases, the customer will proceed to place their order, and in the rare case that they don't, they didn't intend to work with you anyway. Their intention was to break even with you by paying you what you paid your supply company. You can't do this and stay in business.

3. When trying to obtain a new customer, it is always better for you (the owner) to present the company and the company's products rather than using an employee or an independent agent. After you've gotten their business, you could assign an agent or employee to them, but initially, it is always better for you to be the presenter. Many of your agents and employees won't have the passion or the knowledge that you have; therefore, they may not give the best presentation. Now, if you have an agent or employee that is passionate, you can definitely let them handle your newbies. Never send the man making the least out to do the most.

4. Dress professionally unless the job calls for casual attire. You don't have to go over-the-top with tuxedos and sequenced dresses, but you can present your product or service wearing professional attire.

5. Always wear comfortable attire. Let's say that you open a real estate business and you want to show a few people some properties that are on your list to sell. But you purchased and wore these beautiful stilettos that you knew would look great with your earth tone blazer. It's the middle of July, and you're not only sweaty, but your toes are beginning to dial 911 from your shoes. To make matters worse, you are showing properties to a young and energetic couple who are a little hard to please. You've shown them five properties already, and they want to see every property on your list. The

problem is that you have 15 properties on your list, and they are averaging 30 minutes per property viewing! Chances are, you wouldn't sell them because you are improperly dressed, and you'd probably start snarling after an hour or so. Always hope for the least amount of time out, but prepare to be out all day.

6. Never sink to your customer's level if they want to challenge you. You've seen it happen before. Mr. Pompous is puffed up, and he wants his wife to think that he's the man, so he keeps trying to aggressively talk you down. His pride is knocking on your pride's door, and you're doing everything in your power not to let it answer for you. The worst part is he doesn't even know what he's talking about. He's using language and terms that he obviously does not understand, and the temptation is there to show him outright where he stands, so that he can humbly tuck his tail between his legs and stop barking. But you're a professional, and you can't deal with your customers personally. It's a challenge not to do so when you're dealing with such a character. What should you do? You can politely correct him, but flow on into the next point. Let's use the property angle once again. Let's say that you're showing Mr. Parks and his wife a piece of property, and he keeps saying that the property value in that area is below $300,000, and the market is looking to crash within the next year. From your knowledge, the property value in that area is $500,000 and higher, and the value continues to sky rocket because of some new renovations in the area. Mr. Parks is trying to use words that he doesn't know the definition of. Instead of humbling him with pride, humble him with knowledge. Politely correct him with, "That's great that you have been researching property values, but you may be talking about the area three miles from this section. The cheapest homes in this area are $500,000, and the market value continues to increase because of the new country club and the fitness center that just opened

right off Marks Street. If you'd like, I can search for some properties within the $300,000 price range. I do know of a few that I think you'd like." One of two things will happen here. He will either agree to check out those properties if he's adamant about spending $300,000 or less, or he'll stay in the $500,000 area and continue looking.

7. Personal hygiene is something we shouldn't have to talk about. Always remember that your client can smell you (if you will be face-to-face with them). Make sure you freshen up before going to meet the client, and be sure to consider your client before baptizing yourself with cologne. Some people have extreme allergies, and it's never a good idea to present yourself to them as their nose's worst enemy. Ladies, a light body spray should be just enough to pleasantly tickle your customer's senses. Men, a light cologne sprayed on sparingly should make the experience a pleasant one. Always try out each scent on your body to see how it works with your personal scent.

8. The most important pointer is to be knowledgeable about your products and services, as well as the products and services of your competitors. Even though you should never consider yourself a competitor or compete with another business, you should always ensure that you don't fall behind in technology, knowledge, and resources.

Is There a Market For Your Business

You'd be amazed at how many businesses fail because the owner didn't do his or her research on the product or services that they were offering. Sure, you may have a great idea, but that doesn't mean that there is a market for your idea or a demand for it.

Some ideas are just vanity, meaning there is no demand for the products or services, but you may still be able to market it if you know how to. Other ideas present the buyer with the necessities that they demand in their lives. What does your company bring to the forefront, and how can it benefit the people that you want to market to?

I have run across many grasshopper business owners that jump from one idea to the next because they were chasing quick money, notoriety, titles, or they wanted to have a business just because someone they knew had launched their own business. Whatever your reason for starting your company or considering launching a company, you must absolutely have footing. Think about a toddler trying to get off a chair. Toddlers usually inch themselves down until they can feel their feet touching the ground. To keep from falling, they slowly lower themselves until their feet are placed firmly on the ground and they feel stable enough to release the chair. In business, you have to do the same thing. You can't just jump into something just because it seems like a good idea; you have to find your footing. Your footing is your gifting, and your gifting will always rest upon the foundation of the WORD of GOD. Your gifting is whatever talent that GOD has given you. Let's be real here; this is a Christian book, not a book of chanced opportunities.

Once GOD gives you a gifting, there will be a market for it, but you may have to be innovative in your approach to marketing it. For example, let's say that you were launching a burger joint, but you had plenty of competition on your street. Not that you're competitive, but you have to draw business to yourself. Just cooking cheeseburgers and fries won't bring the customers in; this is why you have to do something different with the food you cook. McDonald's was innovative in creating the Big Mac and Burger King was innovative in creating the Whopper; therefore, you would need your own signature sandwich. You wouldn't just settle for one sandwich either, but it would be great to make several sandwiches using your own custom signature sauces. This is what is going to be appealing to your customer as well as your pricing and delivery.

Let's look at it from another point. What if you had this great and powerful voice and you wanted to market your music? Simply knowing how to sing won't do much for you, but get you an applause from whoever hears you sing. What about the ones who have never heard of you? How do you get your name out there so that you can be discovered? You would have to do something that other artists aren't doing. You would have to make yourself a unique singer in your style, delivery, and marketing of yourself and your music. There are millions of people who are gifted to sing, but most of them don't think about marketing their music, and the ones that do don't know how to market it.

I remember meeting this very talented artist some years ago, and I was just in love with her voice and her music, so I Googled her name. To my surprise, there were no listings of her, save a few social networking links to Facebook and other popular social platforms. I believed and still believe this girl has everything to go mainstream, but at that time, she had almost no web presence. Her music was awesome, her delivery was pristine, but where was she? This is to say that you have to place both feet on the ground before you can stand up safely.

Your market has everything to do with your reasoning for creating the product. If I want to make millions selling ankle bracelets, I would have to ask myself, "What is the purpose of these ankle bracelets, and who am I selling them to?" If I wanted to sell them to college-aged women, I would have to research to find out what's in. What type of styles do college women wear? What race is more prone to ankle bracelets, and what style would appeal to that race the most? Then, I would have to look for demand in that market. Are college age women actually buying enough ankle bracelets where it could serve as a good investment, or is it just another good idea in bad timing? I would test the market by creating several styles of these bracelets and visiting a few colleges. I would note which styles sold the most and which styles sold the least. This way, I don't do aimless investing; buying excessive inventory that will not sell.

What if you have a box full of bracelets or other products right now that you can't seem to sell? It is usually because you have not located your market and the demand for what you intend to sell. One thing that a lot of business owners don't consider is that they can create a demand by producing a product that is unlike any other. Let's go back to the bracelets. What is so different about your bracelets that will create a huge stir about them? Someone came up with a great idea to customize bracelets with the buyers' names at one point, but what can you bring to the table in the jewelry market? It takes innovative thinking to come up with an idea that just might be crazy enough to work. Innovative thinking comes from GOD; therefore, you should know what to pray for.

Is there a market for your business? Chances are, the answer is yes, but you have to find it or create it. Research takes time, and it can be draining, but it pays well in the end.

Personal Vs. Business Connections

When you are just launching out, you are considered a small business by the world's ranking. During this period of time, you will discover a lot about yourself and the general mindset of certain groups of people. You will learn to categorize your customers by their behaviors. For example, there is one type of customer that you will commonly run into, and that customer is the customer who wants to deal personally and not professionally with you. Earlier on in this book, I talked about the clients that I referred to as "cliends." These are clients that masquerade themselves as friends trying to get free services, free products, or tap into your information source so they can launch a business just like yours. Well, there is another type of customer that is similar to a cliend, but they don't usually try to make a long-term connection with you; instead, they try to personally deal with you while they are doing business with you. This is very common in a Christian business because people want to save money, even if that means that you have to lose to help them save. A lot of people don't actually think outside of themselves, and that's their hang-up, but you cannot trade their poverty for your prosperity.

This type of client will usually try to start off telling you what they want and then will proceed to initiate a personal conversation with you. They may tell you their troubles and their testimonies and this is okay, but you have to remain in control of the situation. Some people are just friendly and have no motives, but then again, there are the ones that will try to stretch you to see how flexible you are. After they've shared their personal stories with you, they will wait to hear your story, and if you share it, you've just crossed the line into a personal relationship with the customer. The conversation can go on for hours, and the customer just may go ahead and proceed with the order if they have no motives, but if they do, by the end of the conversation, they will probably ask you for a discount, or if they can pay you later. Again, what you will witness me say throughout the book is do not go outside of your rules for any customer...period. Even if you did start conversing with them and found them to be decent people, your mission is to keep this transaction a professional one. It's not uncommon for someone to begin thanking GOD for the connection because they oftentimes feel that you are no longer a business that they are having to go to for services, but they see you as a friend that they can go to for favors. This kills a lot of Christian businesses because it can be rather difficult to walk that fine line between being professional and being personal. You should remember this pointer, however: If someone refuses to do business with you just because you would not get personal with them, let them go their own way. This was not a customer; this was a person that was looking for a personal connection or an unregistered partnership where only one person would benefit and the other would get a few compliments. Many times, the customer will tell you that they will send tons of business to you and they know a lot of people. This is to groom you to give them what they want.

As a business owner, I can truly say that getting everything that you need done can be expensive; therefore, you will find yourself oftentimes wishing that you could find someone that would do things freely. In your mind, you will think that if they were to do these things, you would pay them back once you crossed the bridge of success. This mindset is a normal mindset; however, you should not wage war on someone's finances by requesting free services or expecting free services. To keep your business blessed, the right thing to do is simply pay a man what you owe him.

Keep your business running by staying in the protective walls of your rules, no matter how nice your client is and no matter how many things he says he will do for you. One story that I frequently tell people is that of a man who placed an order for a couple of logos when I was still somewhat immature in running my business. I had rules in place, and I was firmly asserting those rules, but this character came along and placed two orders with me. The plan that he ordered only allowed for one revision per logo and he was informed of this. He was so friendly and just kept complimenting my business and the setup of my business. Anyhow, he told me that he was so pleased with my personality that he was going to give me a tip when the transaction was done. In reality, he was simply laying a seed for me to come outside of my rules. During the course of the transaction, he requested a do over for both logos and several revisions, even though I informed him that he was allowed only one per logo. Each time I would bring this to his attention, he would compliment my business, thank me for being patient with him, and promise that he'd give me a big tip when this was all said and done. At that time, I believed him and was still somewhat chasing the money, so I kept revising and revising those logos until I'd had enough. I'd revised each piece more than seven times, and he still wasn't satisfied. I finally told him that I would only revise the pieces one more time and after that, he would have to pay the revise fee. He humbly agreed and thanked me for being so patient with him. After I was done, he gladly accepted the logos and went away. He did not give me this big tip that he'd promised me. I laughed at myself because I knew that this was a lesson from

Heaven to get me to understand that outside of my rules, I'll be robbed, but inside, I would have gotten my big tip by charging him per revision. I learned my lesson this day, and nowadays; I don't care what a customer promises me or how much they compliment me; I will not go outside of my rules. This has caused me to lose several clients, but these are not people who are looking to pay, so I don't think "client" is the proper term for them; they are thieves. Don't be fooled by the titles; there are some thieves that will email you a big picture of themselves wearing their priestly robes, but if you go outside of your rules, you'll find out that they purchased that priestly robe by robbing people like you.

I know that we discussed this earlier in the book, but this has to be elaborated on because many first-time business owners still fall into these traps trying to cut a deal with a customer. If you want paying customers who will be faithful to your business and won't be a headache, stay within your rules. Otherwise, you will become a personal slave that people call on whenever they have a need but don't have a seed.

Name Droppers

You get a call from a customer, and they want a product or a service from you. They go on to tell you how great your company is and how they are going to send more business to you; even tell their good friend about you. Their good friend, according to them, happens to be a well-known figure. You feel yourself bubbling over with excitement, and you just want to go above and beyond to really wow them with your business. You can't contain yourself as you tell your friends and family about how this person is going to tell this well-known figure about you and possibly send them your way for business. After being robbed of free services, discounts, and extras, they go on their merry way and you never hear anything again from or about them. This happens a lot in Christian and non-Christian businesses.

People love to play on the desperation of many small-business owners. At the same time, they love being revered as a possible hero to others. I remember a man telling me that he knew some well-known figures, and he wanted me to partner with him. I refused, of course, but he kept telling me that if I would give him a logo and a website for free, he would help me to make more than $2,000 a day. When I told my husband about this, he laughed and said, "If he had access to that kind of money, and if he was that important, he wouldn't need a free service." Makes sense, right? Because it is true. If he had that kind of power and notoriety, money wouldn't be an issue for him, but because it was, he tried to pay for his services with empty promises. This didn't work, and he never hired me because he never intended to hire me. He was looking for a small business that was desperate, but I'm neither desperate nor do I consider my company a small business.

You will find that many of the people who name drop don't actually know the person that they are pretending to know. Instead, they've probably met the person once or twice and maybe even shook their hand. You will learn that in this business there are many snakes that try to see if they can burrow themselves under your trust. In the same, knowing a well-known figure does not benefit them in most cases. It's just a great conversation piece, but it's not something to write home about because a well-known is human. Knowing this celebrity or that celebrity won't pay your bills. If this well-known considered them to be great and worthy of notoriety, they wouldn't have to drop their names because they'd promote them on their own.

Please be aware that name dropping is a form of manipulation. Manipulation is basically altering the process to achieve certain results. People try to alter your normal way of working to benefit their own personal agendas, but they can not and will not drop your name in most cases. Even if they did, what would it benefit you? Most well-known figures already have their team assembled and are used to, and sometimes irritated by people submitting materials to them in an attempt to get well known.

"Put not forth thyself in the presence of the king, and stand not in the place of great men: For better it is that it be said unto thee, Come up hither; than that thou shouldest be put lower in the

presence of the prince whom thine eyes have seen"
(Proverbs 25:6-7).

"A man's gift makes room for him, and brings him before great men" (Proverbs 18:16).

As you can see, GOD says that your gift will make room for you and bring you before great men. At the same time, HE told you to not present yourself to the king, but instead, let him call you forward, rather than you going forward. You see, when what you are doing is great, it will be noticed if you don't quit, and you don't prostitute your gifts. All you have to do is the works that GOD has given you to do, and HE will do the rest. Besides, many well-known figures are known for stealing unknown people's ideas and materials. Remember, they are human beings with flaws just like you. Let GOD elevate you, and do not let any person come along and manipulate you by dropping names.

<u>Online Payment Solutions</u>

Paypal

A lot of people complain about using Paypal because they've heard some pretty horrible things about Paypal. There are so many stories circulating about the loss of funds through theft in relation to Paypal. As a business owner, I must say that I absolutely love Paypal. I've had an account with them for seven years now, and I've never had a real problem that Paypal didn't fix. Any time someone I'd paid went back into my account (using my Paypal debit information), I was refunded, and in some cases I was issued another card. The people that I have met who have said they had issues with Paypal were ALL at fault. Their problem was that Paypal didn't bend their rules and handle a situation the way they thought it should be handled.

The great thing about Paypal is that they are free to access, and they only charge 2.9% plus thirty cents of every payment that you receive. Therefore, if you were to sell something for one hundred dollars, Paypal would only charge you about $3.29. Now, this is if you are signed up to Paypal Business Standard. With this package, you simply pay per transaction, and you are not charged monthly. This is a HUGE plus for companies who aren't receiving consistent income. Other merchants charge monthly fees that will actually cripple your business if you are not making consistent income. What if you have a small business that you are using to earn extra income, but you are new so you're averaging $25 a month? Of course, this figure is extremely low, but some new businesses see this or even less than this starting out. Anyhow, you're paying a merchant $49 a month to utilize their services. You have a budget of $100 a month to invest into your business.

$100 Investment Budget
-$ 49 Merchant Fee
$ 51 Remaining
+$ 25 Monthly Earning
$76 Total Remaining

In this, you aren't really earning because you're having to take that $100 from your own account. So you're actually paying to keep your business open. With Paypal, you'd simply pay a per transaction fee, and if you don't earn anything, they won't take anything. This is a huge plus for someone who is just starting out and cannot afford to throw money away.

More Paypal Perks:

- Paypal is used and trusted by millions of online merchants.
- Paypal is used and trusted by millions of ordinary people.
- You can get direct access to your funds by ordering the Paypal debit card. This card is a Mastercard, and can be used to retrieve the money from most ATMS. It can be used like any other debit card.
- In my experience, Paypal fights hard to get you your money any time you feel that you've been wronged. I remember having a problematic customer whom I was sure was trying to rip me off. She'd ordered over a thousand dollars in services, and I'd gone above and beyond to give her the best website and branding out. I even added some extras to the site at no charge because

I wanted to just be a blessing. After I was finished, she began claiming that she could not see the content on the website, even though it was there and everyone else could see it. She started acting belligerent with me because she wanted me to give her some extra pages for her site, and I told her that she would have to pay for them. I kept receiving nit-picking instant messages from her claiming that her website was offline, content was disappearing, and finally that I was making her website shrink. She didn't want to follow my rules, and she kept trying to con me out of extra work. I sensed that she was going to get all of the work from me, and then she'd lie to Paypal or her credit card company in an attempt to get the money back. I was frustrated because I'd put two weeks of hard work into her project. I called Paypal and talked with a guy who was super friendly and reassuring. He told me that because I'd performed a service for her that it would be hard for her to get her money back, and because I'd never received a customer complaint, it would be hard for her to win such a matter. He also told me that if she filed a complaint, they would conduct an investigation and all I would have to do was submit proof of the work. I'm quite confident that she did call but was swayed by their response because she'd actually made a few calls to some external companies that I'd worked with on her project.

- Paypal processes the entire transaction for you. You don't have to do a thing.
- You can easily pay your employees or partners using Paypal. Simply require or request that everyone you work with set up a Paypal account so that you can easily pay them for their services. This way, they can receive their money directly instead of waiting for a check that just might get lost in the mail.
- Paypal is super easy to add to a website.

There are many perks to Paypal, and I've stuck with them for seven years because I've always felt that they were on my side when it came to my money.

Google Checkout

I've heard some pretty good stories about Google Checkout, but my experience wasn't the best with them. Maybe I was so spoiled by Paypal by the time I tried them out that they didn't stand a chance with wowing me. I can't really say they are horrible, but what I can say is that it takes too long to get access to your money, and this doesn't work for many small businesses.

When I'd first launched my business, I had a customer who was demanding that I set up a Google Checkout account because he didn't want to deal with Paypal. I was new and I'd already done the work for him, and I wanted to get the money he owed me. In my newness and desperation, I set up the account, and he made the payment. I had to wait seven days for the account to link up to my card, and then I had to wait another seven days for my money to transfer from my Google account to my Netspend account. I was horrified because I was new and wasn't earning much, so every penny was golden to me. After that situation, I never used Google Checkout again.

It is good to set up an account with Google Checkout and other merchants that allow you to utilize them at no monthly cost to you. This way, you have several means in which a customer can pay you. You will have some customers that will absolutely refuse to use a certain merchant, and to get paid, you'll have to receive the payment another way.

Google Checkout Perks
- Next to Paypal, it is largely known and trusted amongst online buyers.
- There are no monthly fees. Google Checkout charges 2.9% plus thirty cents for transactions under $3,000.
- It's easy to integrate on your website.
- Anything associated with Google works with your SEO (search engine optimization, so it is a great idea to utilize all of Google's services.)

Disadvantages
- Takes too long to get your money.

- Currently, unlike Paypal, Google Checkout does not have a prepaid card where you can access your money directly. You will have to transfer the funds to your bank account.

At this stage in my business, having to wait a long time to gain access to my funds is no problem because I tend to leave the money in the accounts nowadays. So, having to wait a week or two isn't such a bad thing after all.

Netspend

Netspend is a prepaid card that serves as a bank account. This card is really good to have because you can set up your Paypal account using your Netspend as a backup. This way, you don't have to use your actual personal bank account if you are not comfortable putting it online. Netspend is great to have because you can load funds onto your card at Moneygram and Western Union locations. Your money is posted in thirty minutes or less after you've loaded the card. This is a wonderful addition to your business because you may have to load money up to pay for a service or a product that will benefit your business. Let's say that you didn't have any money in your Paypal account, and you've just gotten word that a software program that you need is on sale for fifty-percent of its original price. This sale will only last 24 hours, and to transfer money from your bank account to your Paypal account generally takes three to five business days. You can easily go to a reload station, pay the required fee of $4.95 (currently), and your money is on your card by the time you arrive home.

This is also a great card to transfer money to a partner or an employee if they too have the card.

Netspend Perks
- Besides the perks mentioned above, Netspend allows you to receive direct deposit payments up to two days faster than traditional banking institutions.
- You can transfer money account to account immediately.

So, if you have an employee who did not have a Paypal account, you could easily load your card and transfer the money that you owe them and vice-versa.

- This card is GREAT for repeat customers who refuse to use other merchants such as Paypal. You simply tell them about Netspend and ask them to setup an account with them. That way, they can transfer funds to you whenever they want to utilize your products or services.
- You can go to almost any ATM to retrieve your funds from your account since Netspend's cards are by Visa.
- You can shop using your Netspend card.
- Use it as a secondary or primary account.
- If you have several businesses, you can have your funds go into separate accounts so that you can better manage your funds.

Disadvantages
- Netspend isn't all too great about retrieving any money that another person or merchant has taken from you without your permission. I made a purchase with a merchant, and that merchant went into my account and took more money without my permission. When I reported it, I was told by the company that they couldn't do anything since I'd given out my card information. They said that I could only order a new card to prevent that merchant from taking from me again. (Note: Paypal would have gotten my money back in no time.)
- Personally, to me, their customer service isn't the best. Any time I have needed help with anything, I have gotten unknowlegeable employees, and I've never gotten anything settled with any issues that I had. There were times when the operators told me what I wanted to hear over the phone, but did opposite of what they said once we were off the line.

I still recommend them, BUT...personally, I don't send funds into that account unless I'm about to spend it or transfer it into another account.

<u>Business On a Budget</u>

One of the most common excuses for procrastinating on starting a business is one's funds. In my own coaching experience, this is the number one quoted reason for either not starting a business or for closing a business. People often say that they are waiting to get their finances in order before they launch themselves out there into business ownership. In truth, this "financial breakthrough" almost never happens because one can't expect a change unless they do something different. Therefore, many continue to wait and pray for the day where a lump sum of money fall into their laps. Somehow people hear James 2:17, but they either don't comprehend it or they don't believe it. James 2:17 reads, *"Even so faith, if it has not works, is dead, being alone."*

What if you saw a man sitting in an elevator praying? Every time you have gone to that elevator today, he has been sitting there praying for it to go to the top floor. Like everyone else, you avoid entering that elevator because this man is a little scary. Finally, you ask him why he's been sitting in that elevator all day, and he replies that he's been praying to get to the top floor, so he can go to his job interview. You (like others) would conclude that this man is obviously insane because all he had to do was stand up and press the button. Instead, he chose prayer without the works. It's the same concept for you and me. GOD has given us the health and the tools we need to get started.

What if you don't have any money to start your business? Almost all of your money is going towards bills, and sometimes you're even having to borrow money to make ends meet. What can you do to get your business launched without settling for unattractive branding? Most of the people that I have met all say that they don't have enough money to start a business, but after coaching them, I have found that they can start a business on their income. It's not that they didn't have enough money; they simply didn't have enough faith; therefore, they were not willing to make any sacrifices in order to fund their business. Yet, many of these same souls wanted someone to finance their vision, and you are simply not going to find people that are willing to finance your dreams with their own money. And if you do, chances are, you are going to get the wrong end of the deal because the man with the money has the most power in negotiations.

What if I said to you to make five months of sacrifices? Don't go and pay someone to style your hair, don't go out to eat, and try to be futile with your spending. In that time, try to save up as much as you can by evaluating all of your purchases. If what you want to buy is not a necessity, don't buy it. What if someone said that they would finance your vision 100% with no expectation? Would that be enough to motivate you to start your business? I'm sure most will answer in the affirmative, but here's the truth: A man (or woman) will not and cannot properly appreciate, respect, or feel attached to something they did not invest in. This is why it is absolutely imperative for you to invest time and money into your business.

Here are a few tips to help you do business on a budget.
1. Truly evaluate your income. The average person that

claims to be poor is not poor because they don't have enough money coming in; they are poor because they can't afford themselves. The average person who claims to be financially strapped spends more than $100-$175 a month eating out, $50-$200 a month getting their hair styled, and then another $200-$300 a month on additional items of vanity. Most people often gas up their vehicles to go places that they don't need to go. Most people purchase and waste food from the supermarket because we like to have what we want available should we want it. Nevertheless, oftentimes the food spoils before our desire kicks in.

Cut back on your spending by revising your spending budget on items of vanity.

2. Turn the lights off and save electricity. You'd be amazed at how much money you can save in a year if you would only turn off the lights when they are not needed.

3. Hold fundraisers. (First, get a rough estimate as to how much you'll need to launch your business and then hold a fundraiser to obtain the funds.)

4. Sell dinners. Of course, it would take a small investment to get started, but this is a great way to earn money. (Only do this if you're a good cook.)

5. Utilize your talents. This is where the money is! Offer your services at discounted rates. Let's say that you've calculated that you'll need $6,000 to launch your business the right way, but you've barely got a hundred dollars in your account. You know how to cut hair and cut grass because cutting is your specialty. These professions aren't high-paying, but they can earn you the extra cash you need to get out there. You can publish an ad in the newspaper offering your services at discounted rates. Require everyone that hires you to cut their lawn or their hair to sign a contract giving you

permission to use the photos of the work you've done in your portfolio. Let them know that the posted price is only for individuals who are willing to give you permission to take photos of your work and post them up on and offline. If you were cutting hair for $10, you'd have to get 600 customers before you'd have the money you needed. If you were cutting lawns for $30, you'd need 200 customers before you'd have the money you needed. It sounds undo-able, but it's not that hard; it just requires time and patience on your part.

<u>Your Business's Personality</u>

Your business has its own personality, just as everything that GOD has created has its own personality. How you treat your business will determine how it treats you. If you treat what GOD has given you with care, it will treat you with care. If you treat what GOD has given you poorly, it will treat you poorly.

Imagine this: You are a woman and your husband has committed to spending his life with you through good times and bad times. So far, it's mostly bad times because he doesn't treat you well. In his mind, being married to you is enough and that alone, to him, says that he loves you. He doesn't take you out, he doesn't spend money on you, and he doesn't pay too much attention to you. Nevertheless, he expects you to work eight hours a day, cook a hot meal everyday, keep the house clean, and cater to his every need. He wants to be treated like a king, but he refuses to treat you like a queen. How would that feel to you? Chances are, you wouldn't give him the best of you because he is not giving you the best of him.

Imagine this: You bless someone with a great business opportunity. You pretty much hand them the blueprint, the ideas, and tell them to call you if they need anything. You decide to stop by and check on the business that you gave them, and they are running it into the ground. If that's not bad enough, they are in lack and complaining about the business you gave them. This is far from what you was hoping and expecting to see, so you mentor them and give them time to get the business back in order. A few months later, you stop in again, and the business is in worse condition than it was before. At the same time, the business owner is taking care of self more than he is taking care of the business you gave him. There's another person who is more loyal and more committed, so you decide to just give the business to that person and they prosper with it.

Isn't that what GOD has done for HIS Kingdom entrepreneurs? HE hands them the blueprint, the ideas, and tells them to call HIM if they need anything. Instead of calling HIM, they murmur and complain when the business isn't serving them the way they want to be served. They mistook the whole idea of business ownership. The business was not given to them to serve their own personal needs; that business was given to them to serve the needs of GOD'S people. All the same, they were going to get a hefty kickback for choosing to be a blessing. Too many people want to be blessed, but they do not want to be a blessing.

In the example above, we talked about you being a wife who was mishandled by your self-serving husband who thought your only purpose in life was to cater to him. Remember, everything GOD created has a personality, even your business. When you think your business is there to cater to your needs, you are mistreating your business. You won't invest too much money in it to make it beautiful or to help it grow, and you won't invest time in it to develop a connection with it. Instead, you did the very same thing that Cain did. You didn't give your gift in love, and you didn't give your best to the business. You gave whatever was lying around, and just like you; your business developed a bad attitude towards you and refused to be a blessing to you. In other words, mistreating your business will cause it to mistreat you.

If you want your business to take care of you, you have got to take care of your business. How does one take care of their business? By treating it like a blessing even when it doesn't look like one. Treat your business as if you were its doting husband. Invest in it, spend time studying it, and speak to it. Don't develop a conditional relationship with your business; develop an unconditional relationship with your business. Too many people wait to see the fruit, and then they want to sow the seeds, but seed-time and harvest just does not work this way! You have to sow the seeds before you can even get a harvest. Think about that husband and wife again. What if the husband said to his wife that he wants children, and he doesn't want to have sex with her until she gives him a child, and then he'd give her more children. How crazy would that be? He is not sowing the seeds needed to produce children, yet he expects children to come forth! This means that he doesn't understand that a seed must first be sown before a harvest is grown. That's the same complaint that most business owners have. They say they want to wait until their business gives them a certain amount of income, and then they plan to invest more time and money into the business. How can a business give you a harvest if you have not sown a seed? And if you are sowing small Cain-like seeds, how can you expect your business to flourish seeing that your own lack of faith is causing the very seeds you have sown to be devoured? Your faith will guard your seed, and your faith is made evident by your sowing into what GOD has given you, and then believing GOD for provision.

Imagine this: You are a husband, and your wife is dressed to impress every day. On a scale of one to ten, she easily tops a ten daily. She is attentive to herself and spends every extra moment grooming herself. Your kids, on the other hand, are neglected. They look as if they live below the poverty line. She doesn't cook for them, or clean the house. Instead, she buys them cold cuts and tells them that once they are adults, and learn to cook for themselves and her, she will then cook for them. She claims that once they are adults, she will buy them the clothes they need, and even clean up the house before they come to visit. Right now, however, she is so self-centered that her children and her husband fall behind her own selfishness desires.

You'd probably end up leaving her and filing for custody of the children, right? Even what she has, you intend to take because she doesn't even take care of it. Instead, you plan to leave her with the reflection of the one thing she cares the most about, and that is herself. Now, let's visit what GOD said about the sower who would not sow:

"For the kingdom of heaven is as a man traveling into a far country, who called his own servants, and delivered unto them his goods.

And unto one he gave five talents, to another two, and to another one; to every man according to his own ability; and immediately took his journey.

Then he that had received the five talents went and traded with the same, and made five other talents.

And likewise he that had received two, he also gained another two.

But he that had received one went and dug in the earth, and hid his lord's money.

After a long time the lord of those servants came, and settled accounts with them.

And so he that had received five talents came and brought five other talents, saying, Lord, you delivered unto me five talents: behold, I have gained beside them five talents more.

His lord said unto him, Well done, you good and faithful servant: you have been faithful over a few things, I will make you ruler over many things: enter into the joy of your lord.

He also that had received two talents came and said, Lord, you delivered unto me two talents: behold, I have gained two other talents beside them.

His lord said unto him, Well done, good and faithful servant; you have been faithful over a few things, I will make you ruler over many things: enter into the joy of your lord.

Then he who had received the one talent came and said, Lord, I knew you that you are a hard man, reaping where you have not sown, and gathering where you have not spread:

And I was afraid, and went and hid your talent in the earth: lo, there you have what is yours.

His lord answered and said unto him, You wicked and slothful servant, you knew that I reap where I sowed not, and gather where I have not spread:

You ought therefore to have put my money to the exchangers, and then at my coming I should have received my own with interest.

Take therefore the talent from him, and give it unto him who has ten talents.

<u>For unto everyone that has shall be given, and he shall have abundance: but from him that has not shall be taken away even that which he has.</u>

"And <u>cast the **unprofitable**</u> servant into outer darkness: there shall be weeping and gnashing of teeth" (Matthew 25:14-30)

As you can see, the unprofitable or wicked servant buried the talent that his master had given him, and he did nothing with it. The other two servants loved and respected their master, and were overjoyed to show him their accomplishments. There was no joy in the last servant, of course. His view of his master was totally different than the view the righteous servants had. He said that his master was a harsh man, and that he gathered crops that he didn't plant. In other words, he was calling him unfair.

Why did he only receive one talent in the first place? Because he could not be trusted. Can GOD trust you with what HE has given you or what HE wants to give you or will you consume your seed? Faith is not waiting for the blessings to manifest before investing into your vision; faith is believing GOD and doing what HE told you to do. The problem is too many people are concerned about self to the point where they miss the big picture. It's not about you; it's not about me; it's about the Kingdom of GOD.

Just like money, GOD designed everything in the earth to respond to your choices. How your business responds to you is a direct reflection of how you treat your business. Treat her well, and she will birth out many blessings to you.

The Seven Layers to Success

There are seven layers to success. The world would call them the seven levels of success, but as a Christian, you don't tap into the same realm as the world. The world looks for success on the outside, and they take it to heart once they've found what they believe to be success. The world defines success as having the riches, the white picket fence, two to three children, the trophy spouse, and the family dog. This isn't success; it's settling. But our success starts on the inside and births outwardly to manifest itself since GOD lives in our hearts. Therefore, we must go deeper into our minds to plant the seeds of knowledge in order to reap a harvest of understanding. This is called obedience. In obedience, we are simply searching out the heart of GOD. In doing so, GOD will attach wisdom to our understanding and cause it to confirm the very knowledge that we have growing on the inside of us. In CHRIST, success can be summed up in one word: love.

With most Christian business owners, there are limitations that they aren't willing to cross or endure to find their way to success. That's because the average Christian business owner defines success the same way the world defines success. This mentality is crippling because we place limitations on GOD with our lack of knowledge, and we offend GOD with our covetousness. Can you imagine being a dress maker, and someone coming to your store with another dress maker's gown and asking you to recreate it? They want you to make it because your prices are cheaper. They are basically saying that they want to work with the other dress maker, but they are settling for you because you fit in their budget. This works the same way with GOD. HE could give you a much better success story, but when you come to HIM with Satan's blueprint, and ask HIM to build it for you, you are placing yourself in a dangerous place. In doing this you are basically saying that you want to be of the world, but you are settling for GOD. GOD has a far better vision for you than you have for yourself. Consequently, many Christian entrepreneurs do not and cannot weather the slightest of storms that challenge them. Each storm that you face as a business owner comes for a reason. All the same, each storm has a treasure trove of wisdom hidden in its belly, but you have to rip open its belly to get it. How do you do this? By praising GOD and staying obedient throughout your dark hour.

There are seven layers to success, and each layer has an atmosphere that is characterized by a certain type of weather. As GOD peels through the layers of you to uncover the success in you, you will find yourself going through storms. These storms aren't always sent by the enemy; sometimes they are tests sent to show us what is on the inside of us. GOD already knows our hearts, but as Christians, we often think that we have it all together, and that we've finally arrived at the whole heart of God. Unbeknownst to us, there is always something holding us back, and the storms will come to reveal our weaknesses and teach us how to tap into our strengths. If you overcome the storm, repent of your sin, and renounce the sin, you will find yourself at a whole new level. The old layer of you will have been peeled away to reveal a new and renewed you with a greater depth of understanding, and a stronger walk of faith.

Be knowledgeable about each layer so that when that layer is being peeled away from you, you won't quit or tap out; instead, you will continue to tap into the WORD that lives on the inside of you.

Layer One
Your Knowledge and Understanding

Your understanding is not only a surface layer, but it reaches deep within your heart and grafts itself into each layer of you. You can't get to any other layer until your understanding has been changed, enlarged, and it becomes dependent on GOD. Oftentimes, new knowledge is rejected because previous knowledge has birthed an understanding in us that is untrue. Therefore, to change our understanding, we must get new knowledge. New knowledge isn't always welcomed or searched for because a lot of people don't want to research or embrace a whole new understanding. This is because they're comfortable in their current state of thinking.

This layer is pretty hard to peel back because it is directly linked to our beliefs. We must get new knowledge to get new understanding. To obtain new knowledge, we must search for it, and position ourselves to receive it. You do this by subjecting yourself to hours upon hours of research via the Internet, live studies, Bible studies, and so on. This requires an unyielding dedication, perseverance, and persistence that can only be given to you by GOD. So, you have to pray for it and then tap into it.

Learn more about the business you are in or you are getting into. Learn what is required of you, and how to maintain the business. Too many people only learn how to start a business, but they never check to see what is required to maintain a business. Secure your business by searching out this knowledge. Search out the laws and legal requirements as well. In addition, be sure to continue learning what you can bring to the table that makes your business stand out.

Layer Two
Your Belief System

This has got to be the pit-bull of misunderstanding, and the most stubborn layer that we have. Our belief system is a combination of what we believe in the natural, and what we believe in the spiritual. We often try to mix the two to come up with this perfect brew of understanding, but instead, we get a religiously grafted in misunderstanding that can only be cut out by the hands of GOD. When this layer is being peeled back, we go through our greatest of storms because we are hurt by the ripping away of what we received. GOD warned us to cast down evil imaginations and EVERY high thing that exalts itself against the knowledge of GOD. *(See 2 Corinthians 10:5).* In this, GOD is warning us to reject anything that comes against our knowledge of HIM. Now, you can't do this effectively if you simply don't know HIM or know much about HIM. Anytime we don't cast down words or imaginations; we believe them, or better yet, receive them. They become a part of our belief system or our heart. When it hasn't been cast down, it has to be cast out. This is when the LORD takes us through open-heart surgery to remove every lie and false doctrine that has made its home in our hearts. Oftentimes, our only anesthesia is filling ourselves with new knowledge and staying busy so that we can finally get through and recover from the procedure.

To get to your belief system, you need to pray and ask the LORD to evict any lie that is living on the inside of you. At the same time, ask HIM to provide the Truth to you so that the Truth can fill those now empty places. Finally, you need to try every word and every doctrine that auditions to play a role in your thinking by the WORD of GOD. You also need to try the people who are speaking into your understanding by the WORD of GOD. Compare what they say with what GOD said in HIS WORD. During this process, do NOT give up, and do NOT tap out. Ask the LORD to loan you HIS strength as HE continues to purge you of the lies and false doctrines. Occupy your time with productive and Kingdom driven tasks, and absolutely refuse to stop the process just because it hurts.

During this process, you will question yourself a lot. There may be times when you think you're crazy and there may be times when you think you're going crazy. This is normal when what we believe is being challenged by new evidence and pulled out of us. During this process, many people who are or were in your circle will start to distance themselves from you while others will basically tell you that the new information that is being put in you is misguided. Don't be fooled by their titles and don't stop believing GOD to believe them. Ask the LORD to clarify HIS voice in you, and keep letting HIM process you. The process won't kill you, and it won't lead you astray. The process is called a purging, and a purging is **NEVER** fun. GOD purges us of old information, so HE can pour in new information.

Layer Three
Your Relationships

During this time, GOD begins to remove the people from our lives who have been holding us back. Don't be surprised at who HE separates from you, be it Mother, Father, sister, brother, or that best friend who would have taken a bullet for you at one point. This is the stage where most believers (80% or more) turn back because of what they are losing. They never take the time to let GOD show them what they will be gaining in return. Please understand that your loved ones are like a city, and they can only love you while you are within their city's limits, but once you go outside of their understanding; you can find yourself becoming a hated thing. Only GOD can give you agape (unconditional love), and GOD has to be in them before they can give you unconditional love. But, when they are wholly worldly or partly worldly, their love is conditional, and it has its limitations. Never return to the confines of one's understanding to remain a part of their lives. You may be the very tool that GOD uses to save their soul. In success, you have to be willing to let go of anything and anyone who GOD tells you to release.

Another relationship you will find that is changed is your relationship with yourself. How you see you will change because the lies that you were told are being purged out of you. When our view of ourselves begins to change, we are often not scared by it, so this part is easy for most believers.

Then there is your relationship with money and material things. Now, this is when you are really tested because most believers love and trust their money. They say that they don't, but when they are required to part from it for a little while, they become aggressive and unwilling. This is when the LORD will have you to begin to sow seeds into others, and into what you are doing. Your seed is your sacrifice, and it is purposed in breaking the confines of your understanding so that your capacity to hold money will be increased. I remember being in this process, and the LORD told me to go and sow the $177 I had in my account. It was all I had, but I obeyed.

You will be required to sow into your business substantially. The more you give, the more you will receive because our giving expresses just how much we believe GOD. You'll have to go without the extra vanities that you are accustomed to having. It may sting at first, but as you see your business growing, it'll likely become a passion for you to sow into it.

In addition, you may be required to throw out a lot of old things in your home. This includes items that were given to you by romantic interests and loved ones. Oftentimes, these items were given to you with a yoke of expectation attached to them; therefore, they represent bondage. Letting go of these things is a showmanship of your faith in GOD, and your denouncing of poisonous and ungodly relationships and yokes.

Layer Four
Your Lifestyle

Life as you know it is about to change. Everything you thought you knew will lose its lying substance. You may see that your lifestyle is challenged, and this is hurtful to us because it is directly linked to our understanding. For example, in addition to people walking away from you, you may find that your boss now has it out for you. Again, during the peeling away of these layers, many give up and go back into the comforts of the normality they have considered to be their homes for a long time. But you need to understand that in order for you to receive better, you have to release anything that stands in your way as a hindrance.

In addition, you may have been the most well-dressed person in your neighborhood, in your family, and on your job. Because you are now being required to redistribute your funds, you may find yourself having to style your own hair and recycle the clothes that you have. You won't be the best dressed anymore because GOD is dressing up your mind. To me, this is a beautiful time because how people feel about you is made manifest. People are going to talk because they may see you as a nothing at this stage, but in truth, you are simply being humbled to be exalted. Do NOT give in to their speech and return to the cursed limitations of their understandings. Stay put and know that HE is GOD.

What you eat is a part of your lifestyle, and everything associated with your lifestyle is being altered. During this process, you may find that GOD will teach you how to eat healthier foods that are least expensive. When you're used to steaks, lobsters, and eating out; this may seem like a disastrous hour, but it's not. In all honesty, this very moment should be treasured because you are not only being prepared for your arrival in success, but you are now being given the substance of success! In addition, you will likely learn to prepare more foods and like more foods. This is readying you for international dealings and travels.

Change the channel. GOD will often restrict you from watching certain things that are accustomed to watching. That's because whatever you are watching is communicating with your understanding. Unless you want to continue to go through having to be purged again and again, don't give in to the flesh's desire to watch those old shows. It is the very information from such shows that is being cut out of you. Many people disregard this and think that what they watch is harmless until they notice and link their trials to their communications. For example, you may notice that you're in the purging process of layer four, and are now cruising through layer with no pain. You decide to go back and watch one of your old shows or communicate with one of your old friends. Suddenly, you find yourself going back through the painful purging of layer one, and this indicates that the process has started over again. Who wants to go back through that? After you realize that the process has started again because of your associations, you will undoubtedly obey GOD the next time.

The altering of your lifestyle is not what it looks like. You may feel that the process is bringing you down, but in truth, it is removing any substance from you that is keeping GOD from lifting you up. GOD will often empty us out so that HE can fill us up. If you return back to your old ways, you will find that every evil association you had is ready to welcome you back into your prison. They may even throw you a welcome home party. But getting away from those old ways and associations again will often prove harder and more dangerous each time you return.

Layer Five
Your Identity

Your identity is who you really are, and not who you identify yourself as. As your belief system is torn down, you will find yourself feeling lost. During this time, you won't know who your crowd is, and where you stand. This is because the LORD has ripped away the mask that you have worn for decades. Who you learned to be was rooted in so many things, including your belief system, communications, knowledge, and understanding.

During this stage, you may find yourself craving the attention of others, but any relationship you form, GOD will break away from you. This is a time for reflection, and this is the time where you are introduced to the real you. You are supposed to be getting to know who you are a little better. You may find yourself trying on several identities hoping to find an identity that fits you, but each time you will find yourself coming home faceless. Old friends and family members won't recognize you. Some may even accuse you of going insane because the person that they see is not the person that they know. At the same time, during this stage, you may seem unsure of yourself. Now, if you realize what's happening to you, and you embrace it, you can flow through it without incident. But the hurt usually comes from us not understanding what we are going through and where we are in our life's walk.

As this process nears its end, you will learn to accept who you are, and you will stop apologizing for being who you are. You will make peace with your identity, and you will embrace this new walk that GOD has called you on. Many of the questions that you had will now be gone because the answers will make themselves manifest to your understanding through your situation. GOD has a special way of birthing understanding in us after we have conceived the seed of change in our hearts.

A lot of the things that you loved to do before will suddenly become things you loathe doing. You'll lose interest in a lot of things, friendships, and associations during this time because you will have learned and accepted who you really are. During this time, you won't be hurt by what others say about you because you have now grown into a giant, and they won't be big enough to touch your heart.

During this time, you will feel successful because success has now been uncovered in you. You will be successful in your heart, but now you are just waiting on the manifestation of the stuff you want. It is then and only then that you will truly understand that wealth and success has nothing to do with money and things. It has everything to do with having an abundance of wisdom, knowledge, and understanding that you can tap into at will. With wisdom, knowledge, and understanding, you will be able to get the stuff that you want anytime you want it because you now have the stuffing to keep you level. All the same, you may find that the things you once desired are no longer desired in your heart because when your identity changed, what you identified with changed.

Layer Six
Your Focus

Now, that you have processed and have endured the hard times, you will find that your focus is now different. Additionally, you will find that your focus is constantly being shifted as GOD continues to renew your mind. The things you once wanted won't be on your Christmas list anymore. Your goals and aspirations were once the very things that had to drive the once misguided you, but now your goals and aspirations will be different. A whole new understanding is to blame for your change in heart. You will see people differently, and you will learn just what holds people back from embracing this whole new reality.

At this stage, you won't even consider returning back to who you once were. You will enjoy the peace that GOD has given you, and you will treasure this peace so much that you will stay away from anything and anyone that disturbs it. After all, you just went through a dying process, and your soul will be at peace.

During this stage, you will find yourself focusing more on what matters. Your business won't seem so much like your calling anymore. Instead, your business (to you) will be a tool that you can use to provide a product or a service to others, earn money, and use those earnings to help others. Money will come in more and more frequently, but it won't have any impact on your heart since you are no longer bound by the love of money.

During this time, people will see a change in your being. They will see you at peace and more blessed than you were before you started the process. People who once scoffed you as you entered the process will either hide away in their humiliation, try to reattach to you, or try to bring you down. But you won't focus on them or what they've done because your focus is now untainted. Instead, you will walk in love and forgiveness, and you will know how to and how not to deal with them. You will learn to keep your distance from such souls, but minister to them through your life. Everything that once mattered doesn't matter anymore. Without your vision obstructed by the lies and poisonous fillings of the demonic kingdom, you will get a better view of GOD'S plan for you, and you will be in awe.

Even though HIS plan is before you, you will still focus on doing HIS will at all times because you won't be self motivated to accomplish your own self-centered goals. It is then that you are ready to receive the blessings because you are now blessed to be a blessing. You now see the whole picture and how grand it is.

Layer Seven
Your Faith

What you thought you knew about GOD has now been changed, and you are ready to take on your new business. Every lie that you were told that caused you to doubt HIM will have been bound and sent to an everlasting pit.

During this time, you will clearly hear and see false doctrine as false doctrine, false prophets as false prophets, and every lie will now look like a lie. This means that you now know your FATHER'S voice, and the voice of a stranger, you will not follow. *(See John 10:4-5)*

GOD'S voice will be clearer, and you won't battle with it anymore. You will be at peace with the voice that comes from within. You will be at peace with yourself.

You will be unveiled as more than an entrepreneur. You will be unveiled as a peculiar creature who attracts wealth. No longer will you chase money; money will begin to chase you. No longer will the chains of bondage be found on you. You will understand the entire process, and you will invest into whatever GOD has given you willingly. If HE says to sow into your business, it won't be a struggle or a problem for you. If HE says to sow into someone else, it won't be a struggle or a problem for you. Money no longer has power over you, and because of that, money will be attracted to you.

Initially, your faith will be tried. When my faith was tried, it came through someone I trusted and respected very much. It came through a friend of mine who had ministered to me so many times, and just prayed Heaven down for me. He was someone I could go to when I needed a Word from GOD; he was someone I could depend on in times of trouble.

One day, he began to change and his messages began to change. I realized that he had embraced a whole new doctrine and was trying to impart it to me. My spirit was troubled; my heart was broken, and I was confused. The more I listened to him about his new beliefs, the more I knew that my time as his friend was up. I felt guilty in a sense because I truly felt like I owed him because he'd been such a dear friend to me. I was at a crossroad where I was being called to continue on without him by GOD, and at the same time, I was dealing with my understanding of what a friend is and what a friend does. It turned out that I had placed so much faith in this person, and that faith had to be uprooted. He was just a man, but JEHOVAH is GOD. It wasn't a hard decision for me; GOD wins in my life and there is no person, thing, or power before HIM in my heart. The hard part, however, was breaking the yoke of guilt that the enemy was trying to weigh me down with. How could you turn your back after all he's done for you? My heart was heavy, but my mind was made up. I've come too far to turn back now.

And he wasn't the only one. There were people that I loved and held dear to my heart, and I could see that their view of me had changed. This is because they didn't know this new creature that I was; they only knew the old me, and they could only relate to the old me. But I was in no way going to raise the old Tiffany from the grave for them, so I had to understand that this was part of the process. They couldn't come with me, and I had to learn to be okay with that.

If you have faith in man at any extent, that faith will be brought to the surface and tested. If you reverence a person, that reverence will be brought to the surface and destroyed. If you love someone more than you love the LORD, that relationship will be put to the test and found idolatrous. Sadly enough, even after reaching this level, many people quit the process and return to their old way of thinking because this new level of faith is too expensive to them. They are not willing to let go of the very things and relationships that GOD is separating them from. This means that their old lifestyle, and the people in it have more value to them than their relationship with the LORD. They made it through so many different levels, but gave up when their faith was tested.

When your faith is tested, this is usually indicative of you being at the door of your blessing. Do not turn away, but keep pressing forward in faith. If you continue forward in HIM, you will be a part of small percentage of people who went through this training course and came out whole.

Each layer has certain characteristics that pretty much let you know where you are, and where GOD is in you. Additionally, the order in which each layer is accessed and tried may vary from person to person because different people have different issues. Nevertheless, each layer will always be traced all the way to a person's faith or lack thereof because our faith is our life's foundation.